How To Invest In Gold

How To Invest In Gold

Peter C. Cavelti

Follett Publishing Company
Chicago

**Library of Congress Cataloging in
Publication Data**

Cavelti, Peter C   1947–
  How to invest in gold.

  Bibliography: p.
  Includes index.
  1. Gold. I. Title.
HG289.C38 1980   332.63   79-57161

ISBN 0-695-81423-0

First American Edition

Second Printing

Printed and bound in Canada by Webcom Limited

Thanks

go to my friend Max Layton who encouraged, motivated and helped me in writing this book.

The help of all those bankers, dealers and brokers and the many others who assisted in preparing and producing this book is also greatly appreciated.

Socrates and the Economist

Socrates: I see that your chief piece of money carries a legend affirming it is a promise to pay the bearer the sum of one pound. What is this thing, a pound, of which payment is thus promised?

Economist: A pound is the British unit of account.

Socrates: So there is, I suppose, some concrete object which embodies more firmly that abstract unit of account than does this paper promise?

Economist: There is no such object, O Socrates!

Socrates: Indeed? Then what your Bank promises is to give me another promise stamped with a different number in case I should regard the number stamped on this promise as in some way ill-omened?

Economist: It would seem, indeed, to be promising something of that kind.

This imaginary conversation between the philosopher Socrates and an economist appears in "Essays on Monetary Theory", by Prof. D.H. Robertson—published by P.S. King & Son, London, 1940.

Contents

List of Charts, Tables and Illustrations

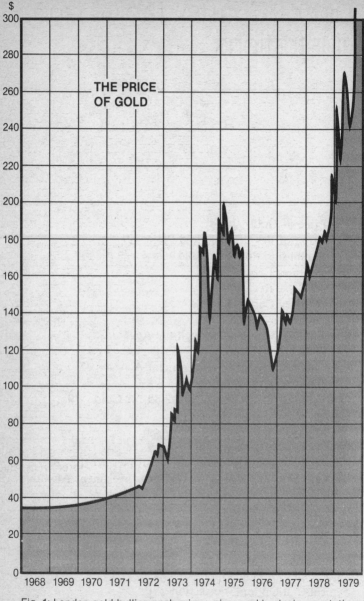

THE PRICE OF GOLD

Fig. 1: London gold bullion cash price, using weekly closing quotations in United States dollars per ounce.

Introduction

Every professional has his favourite stories to tell about his market. Mine are the stories of a gold trader. When asked what they are, I usually refer to the two stories that will probably stay on my mind for a long time.

The first one is about a man who came to see me several years ago. He had saved a considerable amount of money and had decided that he did not wish to leave it all in his bank account, but that he would take $5,000.00 and invest this money in a constructive and educational way. The first kind of investment he concentrated on was in the area of gold. He read several books about the subject and finally decided he was ready to make his investment. Considering his objectives, which were more or less conservative, I recommended that he purchase bullion. He bought bullion in the $130 range and soon after the price was at $160. Encouraged by the results, he decided to take another $5,000.00 from his bank account and also invest it in gold. Soon, the price of gold was $180 per ounce, and his profits were excellent. At that time, he was enthusiastic enough to come and see me and tell me that he now wanted to venture into the futures markets, where he could apply a leveraged investment strategy (he could purchase many more times the amount of gold than his money would buy). Convinced that I was dealing with a typical case of "gold fever," I set out to bring my client back to earth. I told him that I did not think the futures markets were for people like him, and I cautioned him not to use this approach. Moreover, I advised him to sell the gold he was holding and take his profits, because I thought it was at a rather over-valued level. He listened to me patiently and then decided that he had reached a level where he no longer needed advice. He withdrew all his money and put it down as a deposit against ten futures contracts, at that time the equivalent of approximately $180,000.

I saw my client two more times. The first time was when he informed me that he had made $14,000.00 on his investment (the gold price was now at $194 per ounce). The second time was when he came to tell me the sad story of his financial ruin. The gold price had peaked out at $200 per ounce and dropped back very rapidly. Within a few days my former client had lost his initial investment, his house, all his belongings, and the respect of his friends and family.

My second story deals with another of my clients. This investor, a student of international economics, decided in the late sixties that developments unfolding within the international monetary system could only lead to an enormous inflation problem. After serious study and analysis, he purchased gold at around $65 per ounce and has held onto it with much determination ever since. In 1974, gold moved up over U.S.$200 per ounce, and there were few people who did not sell their investment then or during the sharp downward correction which occurred afterwards. Most recently, gold has been in the news again, establishing new highs every few days. In late 1974, as well as during the past few weeks, my client staunchly refused to sell. A few days ago, I sat down with him and calculated how much money he had made. The result was stunning: the return on his gold investment of approximately ten years ago is almost 500 percent, a solid and consistent 50 percent during every single year. Only a few people who trade the gold market professionally could improve this result.

Both my stories are very typical of modern precious metals markets. During my years in business, I have seen fortunes made, mostly as the result of a conservative and determined investment approach; and I have seen millions lost, usually the result of a small mistake, a lack of investment information, or overconfidence. The astute gold investor realizes that for every buyer, there is a seller; for every winner, there is a loser. Gold prices are volatile, there is a lot of money to be made. There is also a lot of money to be lost.

The chapters which follow are intended to help you avoid the costly mistakes I have seen so many make and to share with you the investment strategies my most successful clients have used.

The past three years have been among the most eventful in gold's long history. From $100 per ounce in autumn of 1976, the gold price has increased to over $800.

This sharp correction has largely been the result of upheaval within our monetary system. An examination of inflation patterns, deficit spending, and other economic problems suggests that further drastic adjustments are still to come. As they take place, the gold market will provide excellent investment opportunities. The demand for gold has risen considerably, and new investment vehicles have been designed and implemented to accommodate this demand. To make the right investment decisions, and avoid the pitfalls and danger points, the subject of gold should be carefully studied.

This book will provide you with the necessary background. It will examine gold's evolution and the factors that have led to today's situation. Every possible investment alternative is carefully examined and presented in an uncomplicated way. Different global markets are studied and the numerous charts and graphs will provide the reader with an in-depth knowledge of technical factors.

How to Invest in Gold will familiarize you with the enormous problems that our monetary system faces. Ironically, these very problems are now creating unprecedented opportunities for the informed investor in gold. The few hours of your time spent reading this book may help you save thousands of dollars in the years to come.

1

Gold:
the Metal

The History

Mined laboriously from the earth or washed in the sands of rivers, gold has been the embodiment of wealth, beauty, and stability for millennia. The civilizations of ancient Egypt and Rome were nourished by gold, and through the ages, the yellow metal was the motive for theft, riot, romance, and treachery, and the power basis of those who ruled our planet.

Gold has seen the misery of Nubian mines, the vaults of Alexander and Napoleon, and the vastness of outer space. When the first American walked in space, gold covered the cord that linked him to his Gemini space craft. When man landed on the moon, gold foil protected his equipment against radiation.

There is evidence that gold was produced as long as 5,000 years ago, when the Sumerians used it for the creation of ornaments, jewelry and pieces of weaponry. However, some historians think that the discovery and knowledge of the yellow metal can be traced back to between 8000 and 9000 B.C. They think the oldest item produced were melted down and used over and over by succeeding generations. In ancient times, gold assumed magical importance. Treasured as works of art, golden artifacts were mainly used in religious rituals. The brightness of the yellow metal reminded the Egyptians of the sun, which they worshipped as the creator of life.

---

fact:
In ancient Egypt a skillful gold beater could hammer gold bullion to such a fine consistency that it would have taken 250,000 sheets to produce a layer one inch thick. . . .

Thus, for thousands of years, man used gold in temples, tombs, and jewelry.

Around 550 B.C., the first gold coin was struck. King Croesus of Lydia, today's Western Turkey, ordered his own image to be stamped on each gold piece, thereby creating a medium of exchange whose value was guaranteed by the ruler. Gradually, gold started to replace shells, beans, skins, or cattle as a unit of value. A basis for the monetary transactions of thousands of years to come was created.

---

fact:
Gold is found in a variety of colors: silver and platinum impurities make gold white, traces of copper give the metal a reddish color and iron produces varying shades of green. One of the rarest forms is black gold, which contains traces of bismuth.

The next major episode in the history of gold came with colonialism. Gold discovered in various parts of the globe fueled man's drive to discovery and pushed him beyond the known geographical limits. The Spaniards came to Mexico searching for gold and spices. When they saw the vast treasures of Aztec gold, they quickly forgot about spices. In their lust to steal Montezuma's and Guatemoc's gold, they massacred over 50,000 Indians.

In Peru, Pizarro caused similar damage. He took his troops into the highlands of the Andes and plundered an estimated thirteen tons of golden artifacts. In order to facilitate transport, all artifacts were melted down and lost to the world forever.

In 1792, the United States became the first nation to formally introduce gold into its monetary system. The U.S. system was a "bi-metallic standard" consisting of gold and silver.

At about the same time, the United States became the scene of the first gold rush. In 1799, an important gold find was made in North Carolina. More gold was found in Georgia in 1827. The finds of that period were probably the greatest ever. They were so large that branches of the United States mint were opened in those locations to deal with them.

The greatest gold rush in history occurred in California's Sierra Nevada in 1849. Over 40,000 speculators came from as far as Australia, the Far East, and Europe. Within the first two years, over 2$^{1}/_{2}$ million ounces of gold were found; by 1858, 24 million ounces had been extracted. The Great Gold Rush did not only make men, it made cities and it made California. Thousands of prospectors stayed on when things calmed down in what was then a totally undeveloped area.

In 1859, "Comstock Lode" was discovered. The impoverished Irish miners found gold near Virginia City, Nevada, and sold their claim to a man called Harry Comstock. This claim was to become the United States' primary source of gold for the next twenty years, producing over $130 million worth of gold. In 1876, South Dakota became the subject of excited rumour. The largest gold mine in North America, the Homestake, had been found. With an output of about 300,000 ounces of gold annually, Homestake is still the largest u.s. gold producer today.

In 1896, the gold rush took on even more massive proportions. This time, 60,000 men fought their way to the most unfriendly territory imaginable: the Klondike. Large portions of Alaska and Canada's north were developed in the process and over 4,000 men struck gold.

An unsuccessful "Forty-Niner," Edward Hargraeves, returned to his native Australia. For some reason, he decided to continue his search for gold. His first find, in 1851, created the largest influx of prospectors yet. Australia's population grew from 400,000 to 1,200,000 in less than ten years.

---

fact:
The largest gold nugget was found in Australia in 1872: it weighed almost 3,000 troy ounces or over 200 pounds and was named "Welcome Stranger" by its lucky finder. . . .

The magnitude of the South African gold finds of 1886 overshadowed by far all previous discoveries. The Witwatersrand Reef, nearly 300 miles long, proved too much for the prospecting techniques of the time. It took almost 50 years and extraordinary amounts of operating capital before the reef's potential could begin to be exploited. Covered by millions of tons of rock, the gold reaches from the earth's surface to depths of five miles. Today, the South African gold mining companies produce approximately 700 metric tons of gold a year. To obtain one ounce of fine gold an average of three tons of ore is extracted and processed. From ancient Egypt, where gold was mined laboriously by hand, production has advanced to a complicated system using subterranean pumps, turbines, drills, and even locomotives.

---

fact:
In order to produce one single ounce of gold, most mining operations have to bring three tons of ore to the surface— from a depth of over two miles. . . .

During all these years of major gold discoveries, the yellow metal became increasingly integrated into the world's monetary system. In 1816, Britain became the first nation to tie its money exclusively to gold. Coins and bars in circulation could now be freely exchanged against paper currency issued by the Bank of England, and vice versa. The use of paper money outmoded the metal's role as an exchange instrument between individuals, but gold remained the most important reserve medium of governments and central banks, and soon evolved into a widely recognized vehicle for international trade settlements.

Between the First World War and the 1930's, inflation forced most countries to abandon the convertible currency system. The value of gold experienced drastic increases and that of paper money suffered. Thus, the pound was disassociated from gold and devalued by 30% in 1931. Two years later, during his country's worst economic depression, President Roosevelt ordered a ban on private gold ownership in the United States and devalued the dollar by 41%.

In 1944, the yellow metal was fully re-integrated into the monetary system. With the establishment of the "Bretton Woods agreement," all the world's currency values were fixed in terms of the U.S. dollar. In turn, $35 was freely exchangeable against one ounce of gold. The Bretton Woods system played an integral part in post-war reconstruction efforts. Foreign governments, which accumulated significant sums of u.s. dollars, could fully convert these into gold at any time. However, the ban on private u.s. gold ownership was maintained to protect both the stability of the gold price and the world's newly created monetary system.

In the sixties, the preceding years of relatively high domestic inflation in the United States started to cause problems. Ever increasing amounts of dollars found their way to foreign central banks, which readily used their right to exchange the accumulated dollar flood into gold. u.s. gold reserves reacted sharply to this: from 701 million ounces in 1949, they dropped to 296 million ounces in 1968.

Escalation of the Official Gold Price

1792	$17.92	U.S. introduces bimetallic standard.
1834	$20.67	Technical adjustment.
1934	$35.00	Roosevelt bans ownership and devalues dollar by 41%.
1972	$38.00	Nixon withdraws from Bretton Woods agreement, dollar comes under pressure and is devalued twice. Gold prices soar.
1973	$42.22	Dollar crisis continues.

In order to fight both the War on Poverty and the war in Vietnam, Lyndon B. Johnson wanted to increase the money supply. His only stumbling block was a law which stated that all paper currency had to be backed by 25% in gold bullion. His problem would have been solved if Johnson had simply devalued the dollar and thus increased the value of his gold stock. However, at a time when international attention was focusing on a steadily shrinking gold reserve and an increasingly unhealthy dollar, this strategy did not appeal to him. Instead, he successfully persuaded Congress to remove the gold backing clause. The u.s. dollar, which had once been backed one hundred percent by gold, was reduced to nothing more than a medium of exchange.

But rumors continued to circulate that the U.S. president planned to devalue the American dollar and speculation carried gold prices to over $40 per ounce. The U.S. government and six European banks decided to intervene. They formed the "London Gold Pool," an agreement designed to stabilize gold prices at a level of U.S.$35 per ounce. The Pool absorbed large quantities of gold, mainly from the U.S.S.R., then a heavy seller. In 1967, the pound crisis brought about the Gold Pool's demise. It created such enormous demand for gold that the Pool spent over three billion dollars to keep gold at the artificial $35 level. It was clear that either the official gold price would have to be doubled, or the central banks would have to withdraw from the Gold Pool agreement.

As it happened, speculative pressures became so unbearable that in March 1968, the Gold Pool was suspended. It was replaced by a two-tier system in which the market was split into an "official" segment, and a "free" or "private" segment. The official market, with a fixed price, served for government settlements and reserve evaluations. The free market, in which the gold price now freely floated with supply and demand, immediately became the basis for all private gold transactions.

In the meantime, the dramatic decline in U.S. gold reserves caused a frantic rush among central banks and private holders trying to convert their U.S. dollar holdings into gold. The United States responded by temporarily suspending their right to free exchange.

Finally, Richard Nixon decided to unilaterally cancel the Bretton Woods agreement: he discontinued gold's convertibility in 1971. The U.S. dollar, the world's mightiest currency, was no longer backed by gold in any fashion. It was this event which sent currency values freely floating and triggered a major decline in the dollar value.

By the end of 1974, U.S. citizens were once again allowed to privately own gold. Inflationary psychology, combined with expectations of how much gold U.S. citizens would purchase, drove the gold price to a then spectacular U.S.$200 per ounce.

The following price collapse was equally impressive. As inflation fears gave way to a climate of falling prices and interest rates, the U.S. campaign for "demonetization" of gold got fully underway. The United States, with broad support from member nations of the International Monetary Fund, decided to discontinue, or at least sharply reduce, gold's traditional role as a medium for international settlement, and as a reserve asset for central banks. In line with this policy, the U.S. Treasury and the International Monetary Fund decided to reduce their gold holdings in a series of public auctions. In addition, the IMF undertook to refund to member countries some twenty-five million ounces of gold at the official price of approximately U.S.$40 over the next four years.

A new accounting unit, the "SDR," or "special drawing right," was designed by the International Monetary Fund. Based on a basket of fourteen key currencies, the SDR is simply an accounting unit which does not have the disadvantage of excessive value fluctuations, because it consists of a number of weak currencies, as well as strong currencies. The Fund urged member countries to use the new unit in the same way they had previously used gold bullion. Most nations now hold a considerable part of their official monetary reserves in SDR's and most loans made by the International Monetary Fund to developing nations are denominated in special drawing rights.

Economic thinkers of the monetarist school were alarmed by the introduction of SDR's. In the space of only a few years, the mechanism which had kept in line the power of government to print money had been destroyed. Neither the world's most important currency, the U.S. dollar, nor SDR's, the denominator of international loans and reserves, were backed by any tangible merchandise or commodity whatsoever. Some people began to wonder whether their money was worth the paper it was printed on.

Nevertheless, the impact of the demonetization campaign and the gold auctions, coupled with a general decline in commodity prices, forced bullion back to the $100 mark in the fall of 1976. Within a short time, however, the U.S. recession was met with new deficit spending and a further expansion of the monetary base. Amidst rapidly rising energy prices, unprecedented amounts of new U.S. dollars were printed and made their way abroad. The subsequent crisis, in which the U.S. dollar still finds itself, shook the foundations of the international foreign exchange markets. During an 18-month period (January 1978–June 1979), the United States dollar dropped by more than 40% against the Swiss franc, over 30% in terms of the Japanese yen, and over 20% vis-à-vis the German and British currencies. At the same time the gold price increased against the dollar by a staggering 100%!

Some politicians would still like to see their government's reserve stockpiles liquidated and gold entirely disassociated from the monetary system. But the number demanding a return to the gold standard is sharply on the increase. A growing number of analysts would prefer the kind of discipline which was imposed on governments under the Bretton Woods system and they are calling for a monetary policy in which paper is not backed only by more paper.

During the past few years, gold has continued to serve as a hedging instrument for many private holders. Thanks to ever-increasing prices and rapidly deteriorating monetary values, their strategy has paid off. In addition, some governments have started to increase their gold reserves again. One wonders whether support for demonetization within the International Monetary Fund itself still exists. Several member countries have already dropped the unrealistic "official" gold price and have revalued their reserves at levels closer to the free market price. A most important development has been the creation of the European Monetary System late in 1978. This concept is based on a jointly managed reserve pool which, for the first time in years, includes gold bullion.

---

fact:
All the world's gold could be comfortably placed on any modern oil tanker—that is if any insurer could cover its cargo of $800 billion. . . .

Whether gold will be reintroduced as a monetary standard, whether other alternatives will be found, or whether the coming economic recession will be met by another round of deficit spending remains to be seen. One thing we do know: those few who held onto their gold during times of political and economic uncertainty fared well.

Why Gold?

When looking at gold's long history, one cannot help but wonder why man has been lured into treachery, revolution and wholesale conquest in his search for the yellow metal. We are astonished that invariably holding gold translates into power, prestige and wealth. What is so fascinating about gold? There are many answers. A financial analyst would probably point to gold's reliability as a barometer of monetary and economic health. The refiner and the craftsman working with the metal are impressed by its incomparable qualities. Gold's even distribution among governments, institutions and private holders throughout the world and its unsurpassed negotiability are the most important factors to the dealer. Investors find the metal's rarity its primary asset.

> **fact:**
> Gold does not rust and is virtually indestructible. It is malleable, ductile and has a density of 19.3. Its molecular weight is 197.0 and the metal has a melting point of 1064.43° Centigrade.

The thing that impresses me the most about gold happened back in the early seventies. When the Vietnam War came to an end and the Americans withdrew, leaving the entire country to the North Vietnamese, tens of thousands of refugees poured into North America. These people literally had one or two hours to get their most essential belongings together and whatever could not be carried had to be left behind when they boarded hopelessly overcrowded ships and planes. What could these refugees possibly bring with them? The wisest chose gold bullion. All realized that gold was the only medium in which they could carry a significant amount of wealth in a package the size of a chocolate bar. When they arrived at U.S. air force bases, it did not take long for the local authorities to realize what was needed. The State Department called in some gold dealers who, working with simple scales in primitive shacks and tents, purchased the gold in exchange for American dollars. The gold bars were foreign, made by refiners in Saigon, Phnom Penh, and Hong Kong, and the dealers had to charge for assaying and refining the metals. However, when measured against the convenience of being able to acquire local currency in an emergency, this was a small price to pay.

History is full of similar examples, all of which illustrate gold's usefulness as a long-term insurance against monetary and political uncertainty. The most recent example has been the tragic exodus of the "boat people" from Southeast Asia. How do they buy their way out of these countries? With gold. What do you think they can carry with them to start all over again in a new country? Gold. How do families in inflation-ridden countries protect their wealth? Where it's allowed, they own gold bullion. Where that is forbidden, their women wear gold jewelry.

But let us take a closer look at some of gold's peculiar qualities. One reason why the yellow metal was popular even in ancient times was that it was rare. Moreover, it had esthetic appeal and the only limit to its application was the skillful craftsman's imagination. Its low melting point and its virtual indestructibility made it ideal for jewelry. Gold can be stretched, hammered and drawn to an almost limitless extent.

As history progressed, agriculture and later industrial production increased. Wealth was accumulated, first by kings, emperors and generals, later by governments and wealthy individuals. Gold was again the most suitable commodity for the accumulation and preservation of wealth. Its density is unsurpassed: a normal sized briefcase will hold approximately 4,000 ounces of gold bullion, currently worth over 1.5 million dollars!

Those opposed to a return of the gold standard have often said that gold has no place in our modern industrialized world. They would prefer to see the monetary system backed by some commodity which is used throughout the world and is tied to our supply of food or industrial goods. The problem with their theory is simply that it is not practical. Such a system would enable governments and some corporations to set up huge stockpiles of the chosen commodities, while those individuals without the necessary facilities would have a hard time storing wheat in their basement or oil in their backyard. Industrial commodities are usually bulky and cumbersome to transport. Foodstuffs have the drawback of being perishable. Only gold is not affected by years of storage, is easily hidden and carried, and instantly negotiable anywhere in the world. Gold's distribution is practically universal for precisely this reason. Gold is held by international bodies, governments, banks, corporations, and individuals in almost every part of the globe. It does not represent the interests of any one country, group, or industry.

As a result, indications of political or monetary uncertainty have always seen an increase in demand for the yellow metal. The two world wars resulted in sharp increases in the price of gold. More recent examples are the way in which gold responded to the Thai coup d'état of 1976, the Middle East tensions of 1977 and 1978, and the Iranian revolution earlier this year. Gold is the ultimate barometer of economic health and of inflation. The chart on the next page best illustrates how the rapidly climbing U.S. debt translated into higher gold prices. Both the oil embargo of 1973 and the most recent wave of oil price hikes have brought gold to the headlines regularly. Gold is unsurpassed as an investment vehicle to which those wanting to protect their wealth can turn in times of crisis.

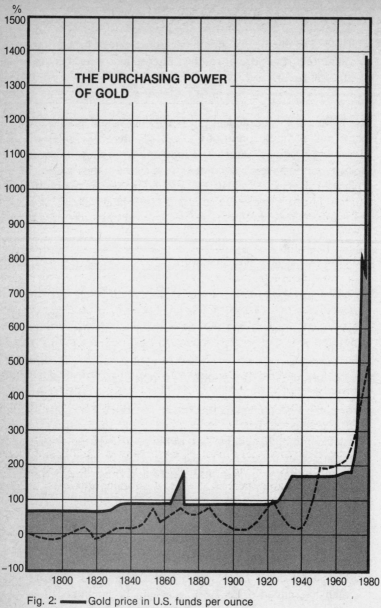

THE PURCHASING POWER
OF GOLD

Fig. 2: ——— Gold price in U.S. funds per ounce
　　　 - - - - U.S. commodity wholesale prices

Gold Compared

If you asked five different analysts to explain why the price of gold moves the way it does, you would get five different answers. There are those who argue that gold runs counter-cyclically to stock market trends. Others maintain that gold goes up when the U.S. dollar is down. A third group will pay close attention to the price ratio between gold and silver; others are convinced that oil, wheat, or some other commodities are responsible for gold's fluctuations.

While there is some truth in all of these theories, none of them has consistency. The only reliable factors behind gold's fluctuations throughout history have been economic and political unrest. On the political side, it is usually the transfer of wealth from one area to another which creates shifts in gold prices. In other words, people may frantically purchase gold in a crisis area and hold onto it until the crisis is over or they have moved elsewhere. The price goes up until the hoarded gold is sold again. Like the price of any other commodity, gold reacts to supply and demand.

Understanding the economic factors is more difficult, because today's international monetary mechanism is highly complicated. However, it is still the law of supply and demand which governs. Demand usually increases when economic problems begin to threaten the value of paper currencies. The problems we have at the present time are all related to inflation.

Gold and the Printing of Money

Inflation is not a new thing. The printing of paper to stimulate economies has resulted in price increases many times before. In all cases, gold was in high demand when symptoms of inflation occurred. The chart on page 28 highlights how the gold price in-

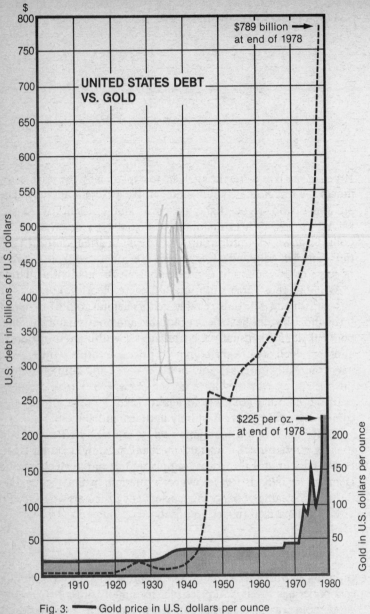

UNITED STATES DEBT VS. GOLD

$789 billion at end of 1978

$225 per oz. at end of 1978

Fig. 3: ——— Gold price in U.S. dollars per ounce
------ U.S. Gross Federal Debt in billions of dollars

creased in the U.S. when the prices of goods increased. You will note that the price escalation of the past ten years is unprecedented according to the price patterns of the past two hundred years. The chart on page 30 goes a step further. It shows you that what caused prices to react upward was the U.S. federal debt which has been escalating to a frightening degree. At the time of writing, the gross federal debt is rapidly approaching the trillion dollar mark!

Suppose the U.S. were to go back on the gold standard tomorrow. At what price would the U.S. have to revalue its official reserves to make good its debt? From the following chart you will see that the resulting figure is over U.S.$400 per ounce. But even more interesting is the remarkable correlation between this debt and the free market price of gold since the official price of U.S.$35 per ounce was removed in 1968.

Gold Around the World

Different countries react to their economic problems in different ways. When an economic downturn occurs, some nations resort to their inflationary powers and print more money which, in turn, is then spent by citizens and stimulates the economy. Such artificial economic stimulus is often needed but can be highly dangerous. The dollar crisis of the late sixties and early seventies provides us with an excellent example in this context. As we learned in the chapter on Gold's History, this crisis was the result of inflationary abuses. The Bretton Woods system, which had been established at the end of World War II, linked all currencies to the United States dollar which itself was convertible into gold at $35 per ounce. As domestic inflation in the United States rose rapidly, more dollars found their way into Europe. Taking advantage of the mechanism of the Bretton Woods system, foreign central banks converted increasingly sizeable amounts of U.S. dollars back into gold. Thus, U.S. inflation resulted in a direct decline in the country's gold reserves.

When the U.S. gold stock reached a low of 200 million ounces (compared to almost 800 million ounces a few years earlier), the Bretton Woods system was suspended. Dollars were no longer convertible into gold. Foreign central banks were caught in a ticklish dilemma. Sitting on massive amounts of United States dollars, they had to choose between liquidating these holdings or supporting the

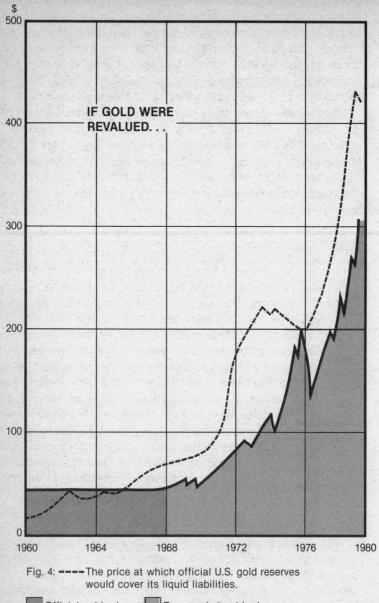

IF GOLD WERE REVALUED...

Fig. 4: ----The price at which official U.S. gold reserves would cover its liquid liabilities.

■ Official gold price. ■ Free market gold price.

dollar. Liquidation was out of the question because the sudden rush to sell dollars in the market would have driven the price lower and created a panic. Certainly it was not in the interest of these central banks to lose even more on their investment in dollars. The alternative was vigorous dollar support. Governments intervened in the market and countries such as Switzerland, West Germany and Great Britain bought vast amounts of U.S. dollars to stabilize its price and hence the value of their own currencies in relation to it. However, they were largely unsuccessful in stemming a seemingly endless dollar tide and, what was worse, they were constantly increasing the size of their own dollar holdings. Even more distressing was the effect this intervention was having on their own inflation rate. Countries like Switzerland or West Germany have a significantly smaller money supply than the United States does, and in order to purchase more and more U.S. dollars, they had to start printing more of their own money to pay for them. This is how U.S. inflation started to spread. In the early seventies, Switzerland went from zero inflation into the double digits. To correct the situation, a harsh recession was needed. Similar corrections ensued in other "strong currency nations" who had imported inflation.

This scenario is now in the process of repeating itself. In 1976, the United States, Great Britain and Canada started to increase their money supply sharply. Within a few months this was manifested in higher interest rates, rising commodity prices, and the gold price. These factors, and a dramatic rise in the U.S. trade deficit, caused the dollar to come under renewed pressure in international markets. Its drop in terms of other currencies and in terms of gold was unprecedented and the amounts spent by foreign central banks trying to support the dollar were immense. In 1978, the money supplies of Switzerland, Japan, West Germany, France, and the Netherlands were on the increase and investors in those countries started buying gold.

The next chart shows you how these cyclical shifts affected the gold price against different currencies. Throughout 1977, gold gained substantially in terms of the United States dollar and the Canadian dollar. Against the pound Sterling and the German mark, the bullion price rose moderately and vis-à-vis the Swiss franc and the Japanese yen, it even suffered. In 1978, gold still did best, in Canadian and U.S. dollar terms, but British inflation started to reflect in the gold price too. In West Germany, Japan, and

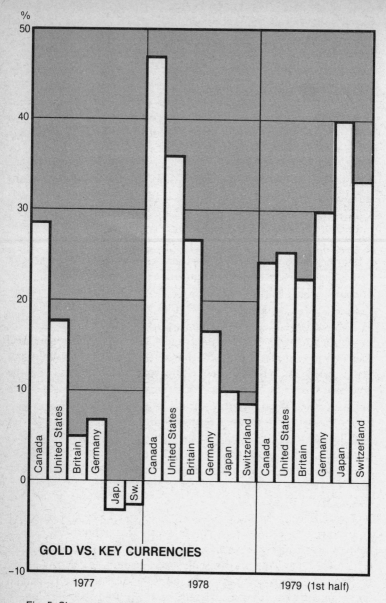

Fig. 5: Shows percentage gains of gold relative to the world's most important currencies.

Switzerland, gold did not produce spectacular profits but performed much better than local money market instruments. During the first half of 1979, it becomes evident that dollar intervention resulted in high inflation rates in Japan, Switzerland, and West Germany. In terms of the pound, the U.S. dollar and the Canadian dollar the gold price appreciated less.

Gold's movements against the United States dollar are by far the most important. This is where all the comparisons come from which indicate that "when the dollar is ailing, gold prices soar." Although this statement is quite inaccurate because many instances can be found where a rise in the dollar's international value coincided with a rise in the gold price, it illustrates a very basic truth: if the world's mightiest currency drops in international markets, then the world must be in real trouble and it is time to buy gold.

Over the past ten years, the gold price has fluctuated but its direction has been sharply up. As high commodity prices and high interest rates forced the economic system into low gear, political considerations usually dominated the way in which decision-makers tried to cope with the problem. Instead of bearing the consequences of past mistakes, they readily resorted to new deficit spending designed to stimulate the economy.

As already noted, this can be highly dangerous. In his study *The Great Inflation: Germany 1923,* G. Carl Wiegand observes: "The destruction of a currency does not follow a straight, predictable course . . . like a cancer, the disease breaks out anew because inflation cannot be cured through monetary and fiscal measures alone; it requires a fundamental change in social and political attitudes and this change usually does not occur until complete monetary chaos forces change."

Gold and Silver

The price relationship between gold and silver bullion is another factor which analysts pay close attention to. Over the past few years the ratio has been between thirty to one and thirty-five to one, meaning that for each ounce of gold you had to pay between thirty and thirty five ounces of silver. Whenever the gold and silver ratio leaves this range, traders expect a correction. However, as the chart on page 36 shows, history proves that this relationship can deviate significantly for considerable periods of time.

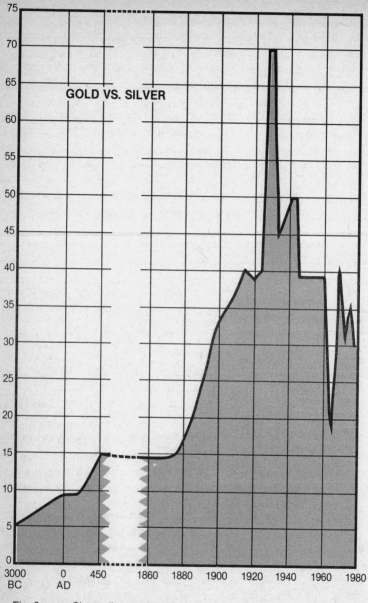

Fig. 6: ■■■■ Shows the number of silver units required
to purchase one unit of gold.

The chart illustrates how, around 3000 B.C., three ounces of silver equalled one ounce of gold. From 450 B.C. on the ratio expanded to fifteen to one and later, when gold and silver together formed a new monetary standard, sixteen ounces of silver were equivalent to one ounce of gold. The discovery of the Comstock Lode in 1890 reduced the silver price so much that forty ounces of silver were now required to purchase one ounce of gold. The next important episode came with the Great Depression, when industrial demand for silver was practically eliminated. The silver price went into a tailspin significant enough to bring the ratio up to seventy to one. (This, incidentally, illustrates how gold usually outperforms silver in sizeable recessions or in depressions.) During the subsequent three decades of growth, the silver price rose while the stockpile of silver which the U.S. treasury had accumulated shrank considerably. Between 1950 and 1967, large numbers of silver coins were struck and massive amounts of bullion were purchased by industry. After the treasury stockpile had been largely exhausted, the silver price returned to its historical ratio of sixteen to one in the mid-sixties. In the following years a multitude of factors played havoc with the gold and silver ratio. Firstly, the explosion in gold prices in the late sixties forced the ratio up. Secondly, quadrupling oil prices sent Western economies on a roller-coaster ride of short periods of high economic growth followed by slowdowns. By the mid-seventies, the relationship was back to the point where forty ounces of silver were required to buy one ounce of gold.

One important consideration in determining the gold/silver ratio is the outlook for supply and demand of the two metals. Gold supply has increased slightly over the past few years, a trend which is expected to continue. In silver's case, the outlook for the next few years indicates lower supplies will be coming to the market. On the other hand, we may well steer into a period of high inflation and low growth during which the demand for silver as an industrial metal would be strongly reduced while demand for gold as an inflation hedge would remain stationary or even increase. Another factor is distribution. As we have seen in previous chapters, the ownership of gold is widely distributed. The metal is held universally by governments, corporations, and individuals alike. This is not so with silver. Silver production, silver trading, and silver consumption are dominated by the United States. Then there are private interests so substantial that they can disrupt markets quite easily. One of the largest silver bullion holdings in the entire world is currently in the hands of one family in the United States. As a result, the silver market is a more volatile market than that for gold.

It seems likely that the silver/gold ratio will stay between thirty to one and forty to one for the coming one or two years. However, it is not wise to look too far ahead in times of instability and turmoil such as these. In my opinion, gold investors should not let their judgement be influenced by the gold/silver ratio in any way. It is a complicated mechanism that helps traders in their short-term decision-making, but it is of little or no interest to private investors.

Gold and the Stock Market

In general, the people who most commonly refer to the relationship between gold and the stock market are, not surprisingly, the brokers. There used to be a pattern of rising gold prices and simultaneously dropping stock market indices, but this no longer holds true for those economies where inflation has become a permanent feature.

The reason for thinking that gold prices go up when the value of stocks goes down stems from the fact that inflation historically had a negative effect on the performance of corporations. At the same time gold, as the barometer of inflation, soared during such periods. In recent times, stock market analysts have maintained that inflation can also be positive for corporate earnings, at least in some business sectors. As a result, on many occasions we have had a rising stock market in a climate of rising gold prices.

Stock markets are worth keeping an eye on. They reflect investor confidence and the health of the economy. At the same time, trying to equate stock market behaviour with the gold price is of little use to the private investor.

Supply and Demand

Major Producers

Gold producers have fared well during the past few years and although their problems have increased as well, they are currently in a state of expansion. Thus, the world gold supply has been on the increase for several years, a trend which is expected to continue. However, the increases from year to year are not significant and have been easily met by increasing investor demand.

By far the largest producer is South Africa, which accounts for approximately 50% of global production. The country's mines have many more problems than the mines of other leading gold-producing nations. To begin with, South Africa's ore is, in most cases, of a low quality. In order to produce one single ounce of gold most mining operations in South Africa have to haul three tons of ore to the surface. On the other hand, the country's mines benefit from labour costs far lower than in North America. The political pressure South Africa is facing, however, suggests that black workers' wages will further increase in coming years, a factor which will translate directly into higher production costs.

South Africa's mines are by far the most interesting. Geology teaches us that the origins of the immense gold fields of the Transvaal and the Orange Free State date back over two billion years. Experts believe that during the earth's formative period glaciers carried mountain debris into an enormous water deposit which was formed in the high velds of the Transvaal. Over the next few million years, this inland sea filled up and the land changed. The gold was imbedded in rock and today lies deep below the earth's surface.

How cumbersome South African gold mining can be is best illustrated by an analogy quoted from a brochure prepared by the Gold Information Center:

Imagine a solid mass of rock tilted, say, at 45 degrees—like a fat 1,200-page dictionary lying at an angle. The gold-bearing reef would be thinner than a single page, and the amount of gold contained in it would hardly cover a couple of commas in the entire book. It is the miner's job to bring out that single page—but his job is made harder because the "page" has been twisted and torn by nature's forces and pieces of it may have been thrust between other leaves of the book. To gain access to the dipping reef, two shafts are usually sunk and then linked underground. The shafts are equipped with power, water and communication lines, and with hoisting machinery designed to carry millions of tons of rock and to transport rapidly a large number of men.

At various levels, horizontal tunnels called "cross-cuts" are driven from the shaft until they strike the inclined plane of the reef. Where they contact the reef the tunnels turn at right angles and—now called "drives"—they run along the plane of the reef. The drives at various levels are then connected by yet more tunnels; those going upwards are called "raises"; those driven down are called "winzes." All this preliminary development is done to gain access to the layer of gold-bearing ore (the reef) to sample it for gold content and to divide it into blocks suitable for mining. The sides of the winzes and the raises are now widened and the payable portions of the layer of gold-bearing rock are extracted. The long, low-roofed chambers thus formed are called "stopes." However, still more tunnels are required. To get rid of the vast quantities of "waste" rock and to move thousands of tons of ore, steep downward zig-zagging "ore passes" are excavated to link the various levels of the mine at the shafts. Rock is tipped into these ore passes and it gravitates to the lowest level, where it drops into steel boxes feeding into "skips" in the shaft which are hoisted to the surface.

Skilled miners are in charge of the blasting operations underground. They know exactly how to break the rock in the most effective and economical way, marking the places for drilling. Holes are then drilled with pneumatic drills; explosives are inserted and the miners move to safety before the blast. Then begins the long haul to get the broken rock out of the stopes and up to the surface where it is sorted, the ore going to the reduction plant for crushing, the waste rock going to the waste dump.

Even when ore, 15 tons at a time, has been hauled to the surface from a mile or so below ground, the gold remains as elusive as ever. It may take as much as a truckload of ore to yield a piece of gold small enough to fit into a vest pocket. At a mine reduction plant the ore is washed, sorted, crushed, and ground until the rock resembles talcum powder.

With the most commonly used cyanide process, the powdered ore, mixed with water, forms a pulp which flows to large-diameter thickening tanks. The thickened pulp, usually termed slime, is pumped to the filter plant where the gold-bearing solution is filtered from the residual slime through canvas filters. The slime residue, now free of gold, is pumped to a terraced slime dam where it dries out by evaporation. Meanwhile, the gold-bearing solution is pumped from the filter plant to clarifying and storage tanks.

From these, the solution passes to the precipitation plant where, by the addition of zinc dust, the gold is precipitated as a fine sludge. At suitable intervals, this sludge is taken into the smelt house where it is smelted to produce bars weighing approximately 68 lbs., and containing an average 88% gold, 9% silver and 3% other minerals (such as zinc, copper and iron).

Little is known about Russia, the world's number two producer of gold. The country is responsible for aproximately thirty percent of global supply and its gold production is entirely under the jurisdiction of "Glavzolot," the ministry responsible for non-ferrous metallurgy. Glavzolot is split up into two sections, one of which directs activities in the gold fields of the Far East and Eastern Siberia, while the other is responsible for Western Siberia, Kazakhstan and the Urals. The most productive operations are those of Eastern Siberia, where the geography is very similar to that of the Klondike or the Yukon. Like the gold mines in our north, Russia's too are mostly alluvial. Weather conditions are extreme and perma-frost makes production difficult and expensive. However, the recent rise in gold prices has helped the Soviets to increase their supply steadily. From an annual production total of 304 tons in 1968, they have advanced to an estimated 450 tons

Fine Gold Production Through the Ages*	metric tons
16th century	36
17th century	45
18th century	90
19th century	4,864
20th century (to 1977)	77,393

during 1978. The first Russian gold find goes back to the early twenties, when gold was found in the Aldan River area in Eastern Siberia. News of the find travelled fast and created a gold rush of similar proportions to those in the United States, Canada, and Australia. Within a few months, 12,000 miners had rushed to the site and were looking for their fortune.

Ironically, Russian interest in gold was reactivated by none other than Joseph Stalin. Having familiarized himself in great detail with the development of the United States, Stalin felt that the same principle could be applied to the outlying regions of the Soviet Union. He was not interested only in gold, but what appealed to him was the fact that fortunes made during the American gold rushes not only built individuals but had developed whole regions. "At the beginning, we will mine gold, then gradually change over to the mining and working of other minerals, such as coal and iron," Stalin wrote.

Nicholai Lenin thought that gold was only of temporary interest to the nation. In his study *The Importance of Gold Now and After the Complete Victory of Socialism,* he stated that gold presented a big advantage because it commanded a high price and could be readily converted into goods. "When living among wolves, howl like the wolves," he wrote. Later, Lenin predicted, Socialism would reduce the value of gold until it would be used to "coat the walls and floors of public lavatories." What today's Soviet leaders would do with gold if they achieved their goal of world domination is not known. What we can observe is the Soviet Union's keen interest in the affairs of South Africa and their rapidly growing presence in the southern tip of the African continent.

* Reprinted from *Gold,* published by The South African Gold Coin Exchange.

Although Canada produces less than five percent of the global gold output, it is the world's third largest producer. Its mining industry has been plagued by declining ore reserves and high costs ever since World War II. In 1941, Canada produced over 170 tons of gold, badly needed to help pay for military supplies. Since then, the mining industry has been subsidized heavily by government. The number of operating mines declined from 125 at the end of the War to around 30 in the early seventies. Even the suspension of the official gold price did not do the Canadian industry much good, although the recent price rise to over $800 improved the outlook for most mining operations considerably. Still, from a production total of 84 tons in 1968, Canada's output slid to an estimated 52 tons during 1978. In our comparison of operating mines in South Africa, the United States, and Canada (page 130), you will note that several Canadian mining operations have no trouble producing gold at a relatively low per ounce cost. Unfortunately, this advantage is offset by heavy overheads, particularly in the wage sector.

One of the primary purposes behind Canada's new bullion coin, the "Maple Leaf," is to help Canada's mining industry. A first production run of five million coins, which will be released during 1979, 1980 and 1981, should boost the performance of existing mines and encourage dormant operations to resume production. The five million coins are equivalent to approximately 155 metric tons, which is in line with total current production.

The United States' mining industry has been in an even worse position than Canada's. The government, while vigorously supporting a $35 gold price, refused to subsidize its gold industry. At the beginning of the seventies, only four of the nation's twenty-five gold-producing mines were looking for the metal in a major way. The others were simply producing it as a by-product of other metals. This is still the picture today. The Homestake, once the greatest mine on earth, is more interested in its uranium operation and, in addition to gold, mines lead, zinc, and silver, and engages in forest product operations. Another major mine, Rosario Resources, has interests in silver, lead, zinc, copper, cadmium, and mercury production. Kennecott Copper, with its major operation in a mountain range near Salt Lake City, produces over twenty percent of the United States' gold output as a by-product of copper. Total United States production has declined from 54 metric tons in 1970 to an estimated 30 metric tons in 1978.

In South America, much of the gold still produced comes from the Andean highlands. The same sites first exploited by the Incas are today used by multinational mining corporations. There is interesting mining potential in Brazil, where sizeable alluvial deposits are suspected in the sands of the Amazon. As promising as Latin American results, which have been sharply on the increase over the past years, are those of a relatively new country, Papua–New Guinea. Rio Tinto, an international mining giant, spent a fortune on the development of a new copper mine. So far, the mine has yielded an impressive amount of gold as a by-product and Papua–New Guinea was the proud producer of 23.5 metric tons in 1978. Other sizeable gold-producing nations are Australia, the Philippines, and Ghana.

World Gold Production: 1969–1978 (metric tons)

	1969	1970	1971	1972	1973	1974	1975	1976	1977	1978*
AFRICA										
South Africa	973	1000	976	910	855	759	713	713	700	706
Other Africa	46	44	45	42	45	45	45	43	43	37
AMERICAS										
Canada	79	75	69	65	60	52	51	52	53	52
United States	54	54	46	45	36	35	32	33	34	30
Latin America	36	35	34	35	35	37	42	45	47	47
EUROPE										
Western Europe	7	7	8	13	14	12	11	19	19	18
ASIA & OCEANIA										
Australia	22	20	21	24	17	16	16	15	19	21
Papua/New Guinea						21	19	19	23	24
Other	36	37	37	49	59	32	29	30	31	33
FREE WORLD TOTAL	1252	1273	1236	1183	1121	1008	956	969	969	968
COMMUNIST BLOCK										
Russia	318	347	360	379	398	421	408	444	444	450
Other	18	18	18	18	19	20	20	20	20	20
COMMUNIST TOTAL	336	365	378	397	417	441	428	464	464	470
WORLD TOTAL	1589	1639	1614	1530	1539	1450	1384	1435	1433	1438

*   All 1978 production figures are estimated. Sources: Consolidated Gold Fields Limited and Union Corporation Limited.

Official Sales

When we talk about official sales, we mean sales by governments or by international monetary authorities. These sales include the gold auctioned off by the International Monetary Fund and gold sold by producing nations or the central banks of other nations holding gold in their reserves.

Let us first concentrate on the producing nations. While it is in the interest of such countries to hold onto their gold and reduce sales during times of gold price increases, most producing nations are badly in need of foreign exchange and are therefore forced to sell gold regularly.

South Africa, for instance, had to finance heavy military imports during the mid-seventies. This led to a ten year low in the country's gold reserves by the end of 1977. Similarly, Russia has to step up sales from time to time. Heavily dependent on wheat supplies from Canada and the United States, the Soviets had to sell gold in order to pay for such imports. Thus, whenever the Russian wheat harvest is a poor one, there is a negative effect on gold markets because the Russians become substantial sellers of the metal. Another factor is Russia's marked dependence on long-term credits from the West. In 1978, when the Russians had difficulties in negotiating such debts—the only resource they could fall back on was again the sale of gold.

As you can well imagine, the management of gold reserves by producing nations and the amount they decide to sell in world markets is important. The release of Russian wheat production forecasts or the announcement of a stepup in South African gold sales can create sharp corrections in the price of gold. Therefore, it is important for the short-term investor to pay attention to such information. On the other hand, official sales by the United States, Canada and other gold-producing nations are not sizeable enough to disrupt price trends.

Information and comments regarding such sales is carried by some of the newsletters listed on page 145.

Central bank sales or sales by the International Monetary Fund are something we have had ample opportunity to study during the past few years. The U.S. policy of "demonetization" resulted in sizeable disruptions in the price of gold that came to the free market. Auction sales by the United States treasury and the IMF

45

were largely responsible for the drop from $200 at the end of 1974 to $100 in the fall of 1976. However, when in spring of 1979 both bodies decided that they would reduce the volume to be auctioned off every month, the price rose sharply upward. What official sales can do to the gold market is best illustrated in the chart opposite.

The official market is basically an open market between governments. Just as in the private markets there are always buyers and sellers, for every country reducing its holdings, there are always other countries eager to increase theirs. Thus, in the past few years, gold reserves have increased noticeably in a number of countries. The reserve figures of some European nations have gone up and it is widely expected that purchases by Middle Eastern central banks will be reflected in their reserve figures over the next few months. It is also interesting to note that gold is playing an increasingly large role in the reserves of many of the key industrialized countries. The chart on page 48 shows you how much these nations hold in the form of gold.

Major Buyers

The demand for gold basically stems from two sources: investor demand and industrial demand. Investor demand has been a big factor in raising the gold price for the past ten years. But industrial demand has also been on the increase, the biggest segment coming from the jewelry sector. Gold is also in higher demand in the electronics industry, in dentistry and for other industrial and decorative purposes. With the exception of Canada there has been a decline in demand only in the area of official coins. However, industrial and commercial demand declines when gold reaches prices which at the time appear excessive. For example, from 1972 to 1974 when prices were on the upswing, demand weakened considerably. But by the end of 1974, with gold dropping from its high of $200, demand picked up again. Whether a repetition of this trend will occur during the next few months remains to be seen. Demand is dictated not only by the level of the gold price but also by inflationary psychology. Consequently, it is quite conceivable that the gold price will increase much further while demand stays strong.

Although gold production is expected to increase there are no indications that the basic stability, which has dominated the supply-

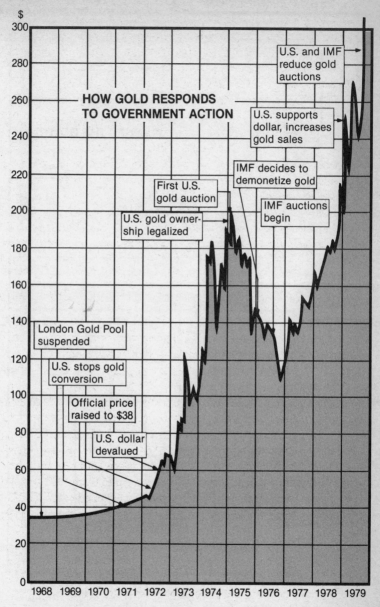

HOW GOLD RESPONDS TO GOVERNMENT ACTION

U.S. and IMF reduce gold auctions

U.S. supports dollar, increases gold sales

IMF decides to demonetize gold

First U.S. gold auction

IMF auctions begin

U.S. gold ownership legalized

London Gold Pool suspended

U.S. stops gold conversion

Official price raised to $38

U.S. dollar devalued

Fig. 7. London gold bullion cash price, using weekly closing quotations in United States dollars per ounce.

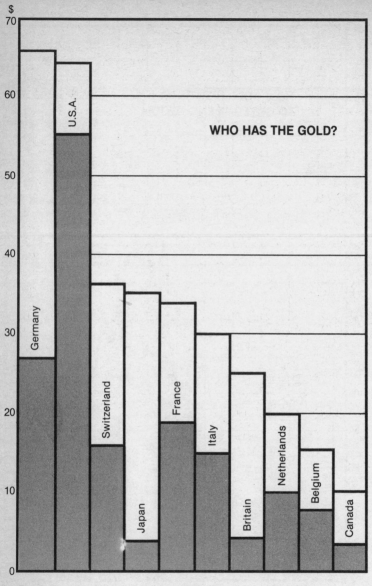

Fig. 8: Shows gold and foreign currency reserves in billions of U.S. dollars as of March 1979.

▨ Gold bullion   ☐ Foreign currencies

demand relationship for so many years, will disappear. True, a nation with substantial gold holdings could decide to sell its stockpile and this would cause a sharp price decline. However, only two factors are powerful enough to create permanent oversupply: either a very sizeable new supply source would have to be discovered or the world would have to enter into an era of economic well-being and stability. Neither is very likely.

Fabrication and Investment Demand for Gold (metric tons)*

	1975	1976	1977
Jewellery	516	932	979
Electronics	63	71	73
Dentistry	62	76	81
Other Industrial/Decorative Uses	56	63	68
Medals, Medallions and Coins	21	47	50
Official Coins	244	184	136
Private Bullion Purchases	159	80	220
TOTAL	1120	1453	1607

* Reprinted from *Gold*, published by The South African Gold Coin Exchange.

Inside the Trading Room

Dealers and Brokers

In the world's free markets, gold trading is in the hands of either dealers or brokers. The difference between a dealer and a broker is determined by their function in the market. A broker merely acts as an intermediary between a regulated exchange and an investor. To cover his overhead he charges a commission. At no time during the transaction does the broker own the instrument of the transaction. Dealers, on the other hand, purchase gold on their own account and then sell it to an investor, or vice versa. They have a position in the gold market at all times. They may be "short" gold (they have a net debt in gold) or they may be "long" gold (they possess gold). A dealer makes his money on the "spread," the difference between the price at which he purchases gold and what he can sell it for. He usually does not charge a commission for the transactions you conduct through him. Because he lives off his spread, a dealer has to constantly anticipate market movements. If he expects gold to rise, he tries to increase his position and bids a higher price than he would ordinarily do. Alternatively, if he thinks the market is set for a decline he may lower his price in order to sell the position he is sitting on as quickly as possible. Dealers in the gold market are usually connected with the banking industry or the refining industry. In North America, dealers operate primarily in gold bullion, gold certificates, and coinage. Some of them offer managed accounts and provide forecasting services. All of them have extensive research facilities of their own. Brokers, on the other hand, concentrate on mining shares, gold futures contracts, and options (see Major Gold Dealers, pages 62–64).

Whether a dealer or a broker, traders handle day-to-day business. These traders are full-time professionals whose job is to try to exploit market opportunities. The trader is in constant touch with gold centres on several continents. Some traders service an institution's clients, others detect market shifts with profit potential.

Most of these profits are derived from complicated "arbitrage" operations. Originally used for the simultaneous purchase and sale of a security or commodity in two different markets, the term "arbitrage" now refers to a wide variety of market manoeuvres. Dealing in a number of different markets allows the trader to spot the chance of purchasing gold at a lower price in one place than he can sell it elsewhere. For example, the Chicago market may react downward slightly when a large holder liquidates his gold contracts. At the same time, someone else may be purchasing a significant amount of gold at the commodity exchange in New York. The price difference is usually very small and therefore dealers have to trade in considerable quantity in order to make the transaction worth anyone's while.

More difficult arbitrage operations are those which involve the cost of lending or borrowing money. A trader might notice, for example, that gold for cash delivery is selling at $290. At the same time, bullion for three months delivery is trading at $299.75. The difference of 3.36% is now compared to current interest rates. At a prime lending rate of 11.5%, the trader can effectively borrow three months' working capital at the quarterly rate of 2.875%. Consequently, there is room for profit. The trader will therefore borrow as much money as he can at a cost of 2.875%. At exactly the same time, he purchases gold in the cash market for the amount he has borrowed and simultaneously sells it three months forward. His net profit from this transaction will be 0.485%, which in large volume is a sizeable yield. If the trader works for a bank, where the cost of borrowing is considerably lower, the profit is even greater.

But suppose sixteen traders of large banks exploited the same opportunity as the trader in our example. The price of cash gold would immediately go up (as the result of an increase in demand) and the price of gold for three months delivery would come down (as the result of increased supply). If the three-months gold price dipped substantially below the cost of money, the opposite arbitrage possibility would exist. The dealers sell bullion in the cash market and simultaneously buy it back for three months delivery.

The money realized from the cash sale could then be invested in a money market instrument yielding a higher percentage than the transaction cost.

Trading rooms take getting used to. Even a small trading operation is a place where emotions ride high and voice levels rise. As the barometer of political and economic well-being, gold reacts to such a variety of things that traders are forced to constantly monitor monetary and political events throughout the world.

A comment on oil by Libya's president to a Middle Eastern magazine, a terrorist raid by African guerrillas into Zaire, or the latest Krugerrand sales figures are all equally important to the modern gold trader. A North American trading operation begins transacting business with European dealers early in the morning or late into the evening in order to buy or sell the yellow metal in Hong Kong.

The World's Gold Centers

Most people readily identify the London market as the world centre for gold. Ever since 1666, when King Charles II gave London bullion merchants the control over gold and silver dealings, English trading activity has been centered there. The Empire's large gold discoveries in Australia and South Africa advanced London to the rank of being the world's most important gold centre.

The market is organized by five participants, all of whom have been established for well over one hundred years. Mocatta & Goldsmid Ltd., the oldest house, was founded in 1684, ten years before the Bank of England opened its doors.

Today, as 150 years ago, the five London market participants, Mocatta & Goldsmid Ltd., Samuel Montague & Co., Sharps Pixley & Co. Ltd., N. M. Rothschild & Sons and Johnson Matthey Bankers Ltd., meet twice a day for the "fixings." Their representatives get together in a room at N. M. Rothschild, where each has a table with a telephone and a small Union Jack. On arrival, each representative determines the amount of gold his institution would ideally like to buy or sell at various prices. When the fixing session begins, the chairman calls out a figure and the representatives respond by pointing their flags down or raising them upright, thus indicating whether they would buy or sell at the suggested price. If all attendants wish to sell, the chairman lowers his figure until some show interest in buying. If, at the beginning, they all want to buy, the chairman raises the figure. Once the flags show that there are buyers and sellers among the five, all attendants reveal how much they would like to purchase or sell. If the totals are not in agreement the chairman, traditionally the representative of N. M. Rothschild, makes a proposal to bring the sums into line. Throughout the session, all five gentlemen are in telephone contact with their institutions' dealing rooms. When the fixing figure is final, it is transmitted throughout the world by electronic news services, by telephones and telex, and, finally, by being printed in the financial newspapers. Although no dealer is bound by the London fixing, the figure serves as an accurate reflection of supply and demand in the world market and is an important indicator to all market participants in Europe and abroad.

The London market functions in accordance with several set trading guidelines. Dealers' specifications of what bars are acceptable, what fineness they need to have, and where delivery can be made are used. Most leading gold dealers maintain a "bullion account" with one of the five London dealers through which they can settle transactions between themselves. It is quite conceivable that a Far East gold trader and a bank in the U.S. would agree on London delivery when trading gold with each other. Since 1968, the London market has quoted gold in U.S. dollars per ounce.

The London market declined in importance as a result of the suspension of the London gold pool. When gold's official price was abandoned, the market was ordered to remain closed for two weeks. During the same two weeks, the Zurich market remained open and quickly became used to the fluctuations in price which now prevailed every day. These fluctuations increased a dealer's risk considerably but, if exploited in the right way, they could also boost profits. Gradually, Zurich picked up much of London's business. South Africa began channeling the majority of its transactions through the newly established Zurich gold pool which combined with the resources of Credit Suisse, Swiss Bank Corporation, and Union Bank of Switzerland. In 1972, when Russia brought sizeable amounts of gold to the market, Wozchod Handelsbank in Zurich looked after the major portion of sales. Business has shifted back and forth between Zurich and London over the past few years, but both centres are highly respected for their professionalism and expertise.

The Zurich market is still largely in the hands of the same three banks although others, such as Bank Leu and Bank Julius Bär, have entered the game as well. While a lot of domestic business is transacted in kilo units (which are usually quoted against Swiss francs), the Zurich market also quotes a dollar per ounce price for use by foreign traders.

The West German gold market, primarily in the hands of Dresdner Bank, Deutsche Bank, and Commerzbank, traditionally offset its positions through Zurich. However, in the past half year, German banks have begun acting on behalf of very sizeable interests in their own right and have thus expanded their business considerably.

A significant new participant came to the market in the form of the North American commodity exchanges in December of 1974. Not that the North American cash bullion market in the hands of banks and dealers was not also successful, but futures contracts caught on so quickly here that trading soon surpassed the volume of European centres. On Chicago's Mercantile Exchange, for example, trading in gold bullion contracts soared from 407,000 contracts in 1975 to 2,812,870 in 1978. This is equivalent to 8,749 metric tons—almost six times current world production of gold!

The North American futures market proved to be a very convenient vehicle to European dealers. If they wished to protect a position overnight, they could simply buy or sell a futures contract in Chicago or New York and liquidate it again the next day. A few years later, this possibility was extended even further when Far Eastern markets in Hong Kong and Singapore provided the same facility. North American dealers could now protect their open positions and then offset them in Europe a few hours later. As a consequence, trading has become a twenty-four hour game.

Black and Grey Markets

Previous chapters have described cross-border trading facilities as if there were an open and free flow of gold around the world. Unfortunately, this is not so. In fact, there are very few countries where the trading and possession of gold are totally unrestricted. In most countries a wide range of regulations governs distribution of the yellow metal. There are even places where possessing gold is a crime punishable by death.

The so-called "black market," where gold ownership is entirely prohibited and therefore commands much higher prices, includes most of the Communist world. In "grey markets" (most of Asia, Africa and South America), gold ownership and trading are restricted to a high degree and, where allowed at all, are normally taxed very heavily. Even in those countries which have a "free market" or "open market," there are usually reporting requirements. Only a handful of nations permit the flow and ownership of gold without any inhibitions.

Fundamentals vs. Charts

So far, we have looked at a great variety of factors powerful enough to influence the price of gold, all of which have one thing in common: they are fundamental. To be more explicit, the factors so far described are guaranteed to have an effect on demand and supply and thus on the price. Opposing these factors are emotional considerations—in today's gold market a powerful element.

Professional gold analysts differ in their approaches to assessing the price outlook. Some argue that economic fundamentals are the only information worth their while. Others ignore them and stick blindly to their charts. Charting has become increasingly popular since the creation of the North American futures markets. This technique is depended on very heavily in the stock market, and brokers immediately applied it to commodities when they entered the field. Charting is popular because it is easily understood and because it is a relatively reliable way of forecasting short-term corrections. Thus, it appeals to the great majority of gold investors in North America who, as we have seen, trade in futures contracts more than their European counterparts.

Although making and interpreting charts is based on the complex science of price behaviour, most of those using charts in today's gold markets follow relatively simple rules. Our example on page 56 shows some of the guiding points.

Once the price movements are drawn up, it becomes evident that there are certain lines which they follow for specific periods of time. In our example we see that the gold price falls from $255 to $225. During the first part of this correction the price moves moderately and seems to rebound regularly from certain points, which follow a diagonal line—the "support line." As you can see,

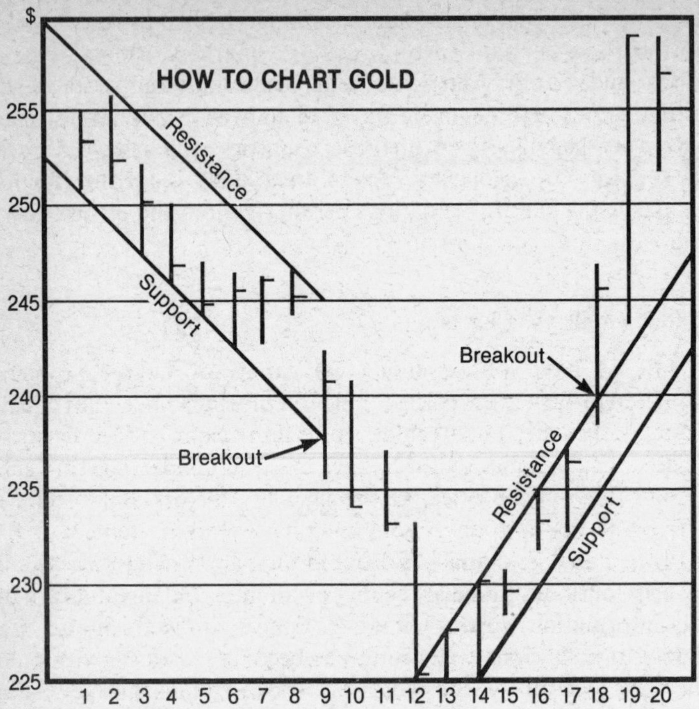

Fig. 9: Example shows trading range and closing price over a period of twenty days.

| Daily trading range ⊢ Closing price

when this line is suddenly broken, there follows a sharp plunge in the price. When a "breakout" from a support line occurs, the chartist will tell you, a sharp downward correction is more than likely. In our example this is exactly what happened. While declining, the price fluctuates and each time it drops two dollars it recovers by one dollar. Following the points from which gold drops after each such uptick, we get another surprisingly clear line: the "resistance line." What a lot of traders do is simply buy when the support line is approached then sell when resistance is met.

However, relying on charts excessively has many drawbacks. To begin with, one has to realize that they only work because so many people follow them and rely on them. Charts are an excellent example of the proverbial "self-fulfilling prophecy." The futures market has millions of followers, all of whom purchase gold when there is a chart breakout in the resistance line which, precisely because so many have acted in unison, can only have one effect: the price will go up. Thus, one can ill afford to ignore the technical indicators charts provide. On the other hand, it is important to recognize their limitations. Imagine measures are brought in to curb inflation and the gold price starts to fall. The price drops and drops, and when those investors who have purchased futures contracts and have held on to them for a while finally also sell, the gold price drops even further. The charts would show another clear breakout on the bottom-side and, to those who follow them, the outlook would be gloomier than ever. In the meantime, though, fundamentals are slowly reversing themselves. Data released by the Federal Reserve and the U.S. Commerce Department show that inflation is by no means under control and things are back to square one. In other words, we have a situation where economic fundamentals suggest a stronger gold price, while the charts are still preaching doom and gloom. Situations like this are not uncommon and just as often as not the charts will have their way—for a while. The important thing to remember is that in the end the fundamentals always win, although market psychology can temporarily distort the trend.

Although I use charts in my trading decisions, I shy away from them in my long-term planning. If the market looks right I purchase gold and hold it. If the price then goes down, I still have reason enough to cheer loudly: the major portion of my investments (which are not in gold) have gone up! This is the philosophy I recommend to all those who do not engage in speculative trading of gold, but want to have long-term insurance against economic and political uncertainty. But whether you are a speculator or not, the following is designed to tell you, in detail, the many vehicles for investing in gold which are available.

2

Gold
Investments

Selecting a Dealer

The modern gold market provides investors with a great variety of risk factors. Investments range from straight gold bullion, for which you have to pay in cash, to highly leveraged futures contracts which allow you to buy a larger quantity of gold for a future delivery date.

Once you have decided what risk factor suits you, what investment vehicle is the most adequate for your requirements, and how much you want to invest in gold, you should select a dealer.

Finding the right bank, dealer, or broker is not an easy task. As mentioned, you need a dealer who has been long established, who can give you professional guidance, and who deals in a variety of investment vehicles.

If you have decided simply to purchase a ten-ounce bar of gold, a gold certificate or a few bullion-type coins, your best approach is to compare fees and charges from a variety of dealers. These questions can be answered by the staff in any of the gold departments of the major bullion dealers.

If, on the other hand, you want to invest in futures, options, or gold mining shares, the situation is somewhat different. You will want to discuss the situation with a more senior person. Be certain you understand all the complexities of these markets before you enter a transaction. Similarly, if your dealer or broker is serious and professional, he will be far more at ease if he gets an opportunity to meet you and discuss your objectives with you.

If you plan to diversify your gold holdings and venture into a variety of investment vehicles, then an in-depth examination of your objectives and your particular situation with a dealer is even more important.

U.S. Gold Dealers: what they can do for you.

Service \ Dealer	American Coin Exchange Beverly Hills, Ca.	Bache Halsey Stuart Shields Nationwide	Citibank N.A. Nationwide	Deak-Perera Nationwide	Drexel Burnham Lambert Nationwide	Dreyfus Gold Deposits New York	First National Bank of Chicago, Nationwide	First National Monetary Corp., Southfield, Mich.	International Precious Metals Ft. Lauderdale, Fla.
Bullion	•	•		•	•	•	•	•	•
Bullion Coins	•	•		•	•	•	•	•	•
Modern Numismatic Coins	•			•			•		•
Rare and Ancient Coins									
Bullion Certificates			•	•		•			
Coin Certificates									
Futures Contracts		•			•				
Options Contracts		•			•				
Mining Shares		•			•				
Research Publications		•		•	•				
Forecasting Service		•							
Managed Accounts						•			
Mutual Fund									

Note: Due to the size of the U.S. market many smaller dealers are not included in this comparison. The table features those *retail dealers* who either provide several gold investment services or have a wide branch network.

U.S. Gold Dealers: what they can do for you.

Service \ Dealer	Investment Rarities Minneapolis, Minn.	James Sinclair New York	Manfra Tordella & Brookes New York	Merrill Lynch Nationwide	Monex International Newport Beach, Ca.	North American Coin & Currency, Phoenix, Ariz.	Republic National Bank of New York, New York	Shearson Loeb Rhoades Nationwide	Swiss Bank Corporation New York
Bullion	•	•	•	•	•	•	•	•	•
Bullion Coins	•	•	•	•	•	•	•	•	•
Modern Numismatic Coins	•		•			•			
Rare and Ancient Coins									
Bullion Certificates							•		
Coin Certificates									
Futures Contracts		•			•	•		•	
Options Contracts					•	•			
Mining Shares		•			•			•	
Research Publications		•					•	•	
Forecasting Service		•						•	
Managed Accounts		•							
Mutual Fund									

Note: Due to the size of the U.S. market many smaller dealers are not
included in this comparison. The table features those *retail
dealers* who either provide several gold investment services
or have a wide branch network.

Canada's Gold Dealers: what they can do for you.

Service / Dealer →	Banking Institutions			Coin & Bullion Dealers		Brokers and Investment Dealers				
	Bank of Nova Scotia	Canadian Imperial Bank of Commerce	Guardian Trust Company	Charlton International	Deak Canada Limited	Bache Halsey Stuart Canada Limited	McEwen Easson Limited	Mead & Co. Ltd.	Midland Doherty Limited	Richardson Securities
Bullion	•	•	•	•	•	•		•	•	
Bullion Coins	•	•	•					•	•	
Modern Numismatic Coins	•	•	•	•	•					
Rare and Ancient Coins				•						
Bullion Certificates	•	•	•		•				•	
Coin Certificates	•		•						•	
Futures Contracts			•			•	•	•	•	•
Options Contracts			•			•	•	•	•	•
Mining Shares						•	•	•	•	•
Research Publications			•			•		•	•	•
Forecasting Service			•			•		•		•
Managed Accounts			•							
Mutual Fund							•			

Note: Only those dealers offering at least three different gold services and represented in at least two major cities are listed.

Commissions, storage charges, management fees, and other investment costs will vary from dealer to dealer. These charges should be carefully compared but should by no means be decisive. Make sure that you are absolutely comfortable with the dealer you have selected. Be certain that the officer looking after your account understands your situation and thinks along the same lines as you do. Take a careful look at the pitfalls and dangers pertaining to each investment vehicle as they are described in the following pages, and see how many of them a dealer points out to you. You want to have your account with an institution that knows not only the opportunities but also the dangers in today's gold market.

The selection of a dealer will be one of your most important steps in becoming a gold investor. Once you have entered into a number of transactions, switching your account to another dealer can be cumbersome, costly, and inconvenient.

Do not think, however, that you will get all advice free and that the dealers you visit will have unlimited time to spend with you. The timing of your entry into the market will be an important factor in this regard. When gold goes up, you will find it hard to find a dealer who has time to spend with you. This is simply because the gold business is a very specialized one and during periods of firm gold prices, the few experts around are in very high demand.

Do not expect gold dealers to have long conversations with you on the phone. During banking hours, they are usually battling with a barrage of incoming calls. However, most dealers will call you back when things are slower and make an appointment with you.

Dealers are not in the business of giving market opinions. If you are not well known to an institution, never call their gold dealers and ask them for trading advice. They simply do not have the time and it is not their function.

If you are interested in getting professional opinions on when to purchase and when to sell gold, you should either subscribe to a forecasting service (newsletter services, telex services, etc.—see our listing on page 145) or consider opening a "managed account," a service offered by a few specialized dealers.

How Much to Invest?

The percentage you invest in gold is crucial. It will depend on your age, your social and financial obligations, and your personal assessment of the seriousness of current economic problems.

Someone who is young can afford to take larger risks and can therefore invest a larger percentage than usual. Someone who depends on retirement income will have to be much more cautious.

A person who is married with children has certain obligations to meet and has a responsibility towards his dependents. Someone who is single, on the other hand, can entertain higher risks.

A person who is convinced that inflationary trends and deficit spending will lead to a collapse of our monetary system will want more protection than a person who simply regards inflation as a temporary occurrence and is concerned about his savings being eaten away by it.

Your Investment in Gold as a Percentage of Your Net Worth

Net Worth Age	Up to $50,000	$50,000– $100,000	$100,000– $250,000	$250,000– $500,000	$500,000– $1,000,000	Over $1 Million
20–30	15–25%	15–25%	20–30%	20–30%	20–35%	25–35%
30–40	15–20%	15–20%	15–25%	15–25%	20–30%	20–35%
40–50	10–20%	10–20%	15–20%	15–25%	20–30%	20–35%
Over 50	10–15%	10–15%	15–20%	15–20%	20–25%	20–30%

The chart above shows approximately what percentage of your total financial worth should be invested in gold. The chart takes it for granted that you are an investor wanting protection against economic or political uncertainty. It does not include gold bought for speculative purposes.

If I Had. . .	These are the Gold Investments I Would Choose
$500–$2,500	–100% in gold bullion or gold certificates
$2,500–$10,000	–75% in gold bullion or gold certificates –25% in low premium bullion coins
$10,000–$30,000	–40% in gold bullion or gold certificates –40% in Canadian mining shares –20% in low premium bullion coins
$30,000–$50,000	–40% in gold bullion or gold certificates –40% in Canadian mining shares –20% in gold options
$50,000–$100,000	–50% in gold bullion and gold certificates or –50% in gold futures contracts (in the case of futures contracts, the 50% is based on the total liability incurred, not on the size of your margin deposit) –30% Canadian mining shares –15% low premium bullion coins – 5% numismatic coins OR –100% in a managed investment account
$100,000 & over	–30% in gold futures (the percentage is based on the liability incurred, not on the size of the margin deposit) –20% in gold bullion or gold certificates –20% in Canadian mining shares –10% in low premium bullion coins –10% in numismatic coins –10% in gold options (percentage is not based on the liability incurred, but on the actual price paid for the options) OR I would place a percentage of my available funds in an investment management account, and invest the remaining portion in a vehicle which appeals to me because I know it well or it does not require much of my time.

The chart on page 67 goes a step further. Having assessed how much you should invest in gold, you want to know which investment vehicle is the most suitable for that amount.

Again, the chart on page 67 is not intended as a guide for speculation. Any risk capital which you wish to place in gold should be invested on the basis of the many opportunities outlined in the rest of this section.

Gold Bullion

Bullion is probably the most secure investment in the gold sector. It is regarded by many dealers as a sound long-term investment and a valid hedge against inflation. In the United States and Canada bullion is, in most cases, the most inexpensive way to hold gold.

Bullion is produced in the form of wafers or bars. When you purchase bullion, make absolutely sure that you purchase a product made by those refiners recognized the world over. Up to date

advantages:	Inexpensive (commissions and related charges are minimal). Instant convertibility into cash. Negotiable internationally. The most direct investment in gold. No sales tax in most provinces and states. Price is widely quoted.
disadvantages:	Storage risk. Money tie-up.
opportunities and pitfalls:	Save on bar charges by buying as large a unit as you can afford. Avoid bars made by refiners who are not internationally recognized.

listings can be found under "Acceptable Refiners" (page 138) and "Former Refiners" (page 141). Wafers and bars produced by such refiners are readily purchased back by all major dealers. If you do purchase bullion made by banks or refiners not internationally recognized, certain dealers will often charge you a fee to assay the gold when you resell it. In the United States assay charges are payable on most bars—even those produced by recognized refiners. A few dealers have started to market smaller bars in sealed packages. Along with the gold these contain an authenticity certificate which is self-destructive if the package is opened.

Gold wafers and bars carry a multitude of information stamped on them. The refiner numbers the bars, confirms the fineness (the number of parts of fine gold contained in an alloy), and usually stamps it with his name or logo. Often the word "gold" appears on the bar as well.

The purest bullion available is gold with a fineness of .9999, or as the experts call it, "four nines fine gold," Don't expect to always find gold of this fineness—very often it is just not available. Between banks and in the retail business, a fineness of .995 or better is generally acceptable.

If you purchase gold of a fineness of less than .999 the dealer takes that into account. For instance, if you purchase a ten ounce bar of gold with a fineness of .9999 when the gold price is at $300

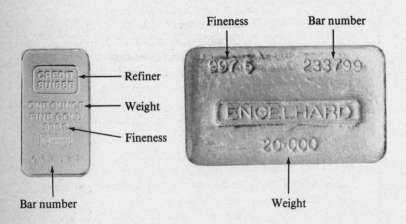

Markings on a one ounce wafer   Markings on a twenty ounce bar per ounce, you will end up paying a base price of $3,000. However, if the bar you purchase has a fineness of .996, you will only pay $298.80 per ounce, or $2,988 for your bar ($300 x 0.996 = $298.80). Similarly, the dealer will discount a lower grade bar when you sell it back to him. Therefore, it does not matter exactly how fine the bullion you purchase is, provided it is finer than .995.

All gold bars (except the standard 400 ounce bars) are subject to manufacturing or so-called "bar charges." Most people cannot afford a 400 ounce bar which at the time of writing retails at over $160,000. These bars are used for settlement of transactions between governments, banks and large institutions. However, "bar charges" are an important factor. You can save money by buying as large a bar as you can afford. Generally, it will cost the refiner the same amount of money to manufacture the ten-ounce bar as it costs him to make a one-ounce bar. Consequently, if you purchase ten one-ounce bars, you will pay this charge ten times while if you buy one ten-ounce bar you only pay once. Currently, bar charges are approximately as follows:

100 ounce bars	50 cents per ounce
1 kilo (32.15 ounces)	80 cents per ounce
10 ounce bars	$1.50 per ounce
5 ounce bars	$2.25 per ounce
2 ounce wafers	$3.50 per ounce
1 ounce wafer	$5.00

A number of investors do not believe in saving money on bar charges. Their concern is that gold will prove to be the ultimate monetary standard in times of crisis and uncertainty. Believing this, they want to make sure that they will be able to use gold as a means of payment. Therefore, they prefer to have their holdings in small denominations and do not mind paying slightly more for this privilege.

Sales tax legislation should be carefully considered when purchasing gold bullion. Contact your broker or dealer for more information.

Bullion Certificates

A number of banking institutions and dealers issue bullion certificates (see listings on pages 62 and 64). Certificates provide the practical investor with a means of avoiding the inherent risk of

advantages:	Inexpensive. Highly liquid. No storage risk. You invest only in gold. No sales tax in most states and provinces. The bullion price is quoted widely.
disadvantages:	Money tie-up. Most certificate issuers reserve the right to a few days' notice if you want delivery of the gold. This right is rarely exercised.
opportunities and pitfalls:	Some certificate issuers do not charge you manufacturing costs (bar charges)—take advantage of this. Avoid certificates which are not negotiable at dealers other than the issuer.

storing gold bullion. In return for keeping the bullion for you, the institution charges you a modest storage fee. For those investors who do not have a safety deposit box or do not wish to place bullion in it, certificates provide an interesting alternative. In most cases, certificates retail for a minimum of ten ounces of gold. The issuing institution registers the bullion certificate in your name and hands it over to you. The certificates generally state that you have the right to demand at any time the actual gold you have purchased. Alternatively, you can cash in the certificate and obtain the market value of your investment.

Gold bullion certificates differ slightly from one institution to another. You should compare carefully and choose the one you like best. In most cases, the issuing institution charges a commission. In the United States, commissions generally range from 1% to 5%. Most institutions currently charge storage fees, which are more or less identical. In some cases, you do not need to pay bar charges at the time of purchase, but only if and when you present the certificate for actual delivery of the gold.

Some dealers also offer certificates drawn on a foreign location. In other words, you can take delivery of the gold in market centers outside the United States.

Bullion Accounts

A number of foreign banks offer so-called bullion accounts, or "claim accounts." These are simply accounts denominated in ounces of gold. As in the case of certificates, the bank at which you hold the account guarantees the gold and guarantees that it is insured.

However, gold bullion accounts are usually quite expensive to operate. A minimum of 100 ounces is common and a number of foreign banks charge up to 1% of the total value of each transac-

advantages:	High liquidity. Direct investment in gold. No storage risk.
disadvantages:	Usually expensive to operate. Restricted negotiability (usually negotiable only through the bank or dealer where the account is held). Money tie-up.
opportunities and pitfalls:	Avoid bullion accounts which do not allow for delivery. Avoid countries where delivery from a bullion account is met with taxation. Check buying and selling commissions and other charges beforehand.

tion. If you do deal in amounts of 100 ounces, these are charges you can easily avoid, or at least significantly reduce, by sticking to gold bullion or gold certificates.

Another problem with gold accounts is delivery. In some countries, it is not even possible to take delivery of the gold from the bank at which you purchased it. In other cases sales taxes, value added taxes, excise taxes or other government fees are payable if you take delivery of the bullion.

Bullion Coins

Coins are by far the most confusing sector in the gold investment arena. While the value of a gold bar falls and rises according to the fluctuations of the basic bullion price, many additional factors determine coin prices. The most important consideration is the "premium" on the price of a specific coin. This premium reflects the difference between the gold contained in a coin and the selling price of the coin.

advantages:	Relatively inexpensive.
	Instant convertibility into cash.
	Negotiable internationally.
	You invest only in gold.
	Bullion coin prices are quoted widely.
disadvantages:	Storage risk.
	Money tie-up.
	Premiums make most coins more expensive than bullion.
	Sales tax in some provinces and states.
opportunities and pitfalls:	Compare premiums and see which of the major bullion coins sells the lowest over gold content.
	Make sure the coins you get are not damaged.

The lowest premiums are those on bullion coins. These coins have no numismatic value and therefore you are not required to have extensive knowledge about them. Today's bullion coins are produced in large quantities by countries guaranteeing their gold content. Some countries, such as Mexico, Hungary, and Austria, have decided to mint "restrikes" which feature the design of a coin that once was used as legal tender. In other cases, such as South Africa, a new design is used or the more recent date of issue is printed onto the coin. Currently, Austria, Hungary, Mexico, Russia, and South Africa are the major issuers of bullion coins. The Canadian government will join the ranks of bullion coin producers with the minting of the "Gold Maple Leaf."

The South African Krugerrand was first minted in 1967; since then, Krugerrand sales have passed the twenty million mark. The Krugerrand's price throughout the world is based directly on the price of gold bullion and the Krugerrand is possibly today's most negotiable gold vehicle.

Bullion type coins are as safe and sound an investment as bullion itself. However, in Canada they are usually more expensive. Premiums on bullion coins vary considerably and the table on page 78 shows you the traditional premium range for each coin. When purchasing bullion coins, phone a dealer and compare the current premiums. You should also determine how much of the premium is paid back to you when you sell the coin. Usually, the dealer will refund a reasonable portion of the premium, although you should not count on it because this depends mainly on supply and demand.

In the United States, a complex system of state taxes governs the sale of gold coins. You should contact your broker or dealer for details before you make any commitments.

Some bullion coins carry a face value and others do not. Canada's new coin, for instance, will have "fifty dollars" stamped on it, which provides a certain protection against an excessive decline in the gold price. However, given its selling price, this is a rather insignificant factor.

Popular Bullion-Type Coins

Coin	Historic Prem. Range (World)	Recent Prem. Range (Canada)	Gold Content (Ounces)
Austria 100 Corona	8–20%	1–2.5%	.9802
Canada "Maple Leaf"	To be released fall 1979	Planned prem. 5%	1.0000
Hungary 100 Corona	8–20%	1.5–3.5%	.9802
Mexico 50 Pesos	12–25%	3.5–5.5%	1.2057
Russia "Chevronetz"	6–12%	10–15%	.2488
South Africa "Krugerrand"	6–15%	4–%	1.0000

Most bullion coins are of a weight which can easily be equated to the current gold price. For instance, the Austrian 100 Corona, the Hungarian 100 Corona and the Mexican 50 peso coins are all very close to the one ounce weight. The Russian Chervonetz weighs almost one-quarter ounce. The South African Krugerrand and the Canadian Maple Leaf Gold coin weigh exactly one troy ounce.

Bullion coins, as all other coins, should be handled carefully. You should not scratch them, dent them or nick them. To be on the safe side, it is best to leave them in their original wrapping. You will always get back the basic gold value of your investment, but if the coins are in bad shape when you return them, you may not get any recognition for the premium you have paid. Moreover, because the dealer cannot sell the coins again once they are damaged, he may deduct from your proceeds a hefty refining charge.

Austria 100 Corona

Mexico 50 Pesos

Russia Chervonets

South Africa Krugerrand

Coin Certificates

Only a few dealers have a reasonable range of coin certificates available. These certificates are usually issued exclusively for bullion type coins, such as the Krugerrand, the Austrian 100

advantages:	Relatively inexpensive. Liquid. You invest only in gold. No storage risk. Bullion coin prices are widely quoted.
disadvantages:	Money tie-up. Premiums make coins more expensive than bullion. Sales tax in some states and provinces. Most certificate issuers reserve the right to a few days' notice if you want to take delivery of the coins (this right is rarely exercised).
opportunities and pitfalls:	Compare premiums: see which bullion coin sells the lowest over its gold content. Avoid certificates which are not negotiable at dealers other than the issuer.

Corona or the Mexican Peso. The new Canadian Maple Leaf coin will probably also be available in certificate form.

The advantages and regulations pertaining to bullion coin certificates are the same as those applying to bullion certificates. (See page 72).

Numismatic Coins

As we have seen, bullion coins are usually produced in large quantities and kept in uncirculated condition. In other words, their purpose is to provide the investor with all the advantages of bullion with the additional appeal of a coin.

Numismatic coins, on the other hand, are governed by four major factors:

1. Their rarity
2. Their age
3. The quantity originally produced
4. Their condition.

Numismatic dealers' inventories may range from items minted in 550 B.C. to modern times. In recent years governments have increasingly issued coins to commemorate events in their history. Numismatic coins are collected for their beauty, historical significance, investment value and educational value.

Numismatic coins do depend on the price of gold to a degree, although it is usually a minor factor. Their premiums are traditionally far higher than those of bullion type coins and their values fluctuate to a much wider extent. For example, a $5 gold piece may contain $60 worth of gold and may sell for as much as $700.

The minimum you can recover from numismatic coin investment is always either its face value or its metal content. You will soon learn, however, that most coins sell very substantially above their face value and above their metal content. Every now and then new coins are released of which this is not true. In 1978, for instance, the Hong Kong government struck its "Year of the Goat" coin. As

Great Britain Sovereign

Canada Year of the Child

France 20 Francs

Switzerland Vreneli

advantages:	Coins have more appeal and are more interesting than bullion.
disadvantages:	More knowledge is required. High premiums. You invest in more than just gold. Not always readily negotiable. Money tie-up. Storage risk. Taxable in some states and provinces. Prices are not quoted widely.
opportunities and pitfalls:	Deal strictly with reputable and well-established institutions. Unless you are an expert numismatist, avoid responding to "coin column ads." Avoid private issues and medallions for investment purposes.

a result of the U.S. dollar crisis, the face value of the HK $1,000 rose rapidly and within a short time the coin was trading at a premium of only 10% over face value. This is an example of how a coin issued by a foreign country can be subjected to very wide premium fluctuation which can translate into attractive gains.

In the numismatic sector, probably more than anywhere else, the selection of a reputable and long-established dealer is essential. The numismatic field is a complicated one and requires a high degree of expertise and knowledge. To begin with, determining the "grading" or condition of a numismatic coin is a difficult task.

Below is a listing of the most important gradings:

1. *Proof*
   Coins struck specially in small numbers for investment, presentations, and other purposes. These coins are usually struck twice ("double-struck") and as a result have a high, mirror-like finish. Due to the small number produced and the great demand

among collectors, proof coins usually sell at a considerably higher price than the standard issue.

2. *Brilliant Uncirculated (B.U. or U & C)*
These coins are struck on regular dies, although they are not intended for circulation. Most bullion type coins and most numismatic coins produced today remain in brilliant uncirculated condition. In other words, their holders try deliberately not to damage the coins in order not to reduce their investment value.

3. *Extremely Fine (E.S.) or Extra Fine (X.S.)*
These coins are slightly circulated and show some signs of wear, but still have their original polish.

4. *Very Fine (V.F.)*
Details and design are still clearly marked; only the highest surfaces are worn down slightly.

5. *Fine (F.)*
Coins which have been circulated and show definite signs of wear, especially on the finer parts of the image. However, all the details are visible. The grading "fine" is the minimum standard for coin collectors.

6. *Very Good (V.G.)*
The inscriptions and design are still clear and bold, but worn.

7. *Good (G.)*
Design and inscriptions are readable but quite worn.

8. *Fair (F.)*
Features are still identifiable but not easily readable.

9. *Mediocre (M.)*
Very worn or damaged.

10. *Poor (P.)*
Unless it is very rare, a coin in "poor" condition usually doesn't fetch more than the value of the metal it contains.

While a numismatic collection promises to intrigue you for many years, you must remember that it is not a direct investment in gold. The market for numismatics has increased considerably over the past ten years and many of the coins are highly priced at this time. If you do invest in numismatics, you should remember that you will accept it as a hobby before long. You may feel emotional about your collection after a few years and one should never mix emotions with investments.

As mentioned, numismatic coins involve considerable premiums over their actual gold content. It is not fair to point out high premiums with many of the older issues, because they are and should be recognized for their considerable rarity. On the other hand, when you invest in numismatic coins of recent years, you should carefully consider premiums. A complete listing of the world's gold coins can be found starting on page 147.

Other Numismatic Items

One area requiring particular expertise is that of ancient coins. Such coins date to as early as 550 B.C. and were issued by Byzantine, Egyptian, Greek, Roman, and other rulers.

Perhaps an illustration of how coinage was produced in ancient times serves best to highlight the problems which are connected with trading today. In the case of Greece, for example, a "coin maker's shop" normally accommodated about thirty craftsmen. The master would teach his assistants how to etch an image into stone, which could then serve as a coin die. For each coin, two stone images were needed, representing the two sides of the coin. When the dies were prepared, the coin striker would fill the bottom half with an alloy, carefully place the other half on top and deal the die a sharp blow with a hammer. Each die lasted for fifty or one hundred coins and then broke. Because the die makers worked with a fine chisel and hammer, size and design varied considerably. Through the centuries, the vast majority of ancient coins were lost and only a few examples survive. Today these coins sell at extremely high premiums. Coins which have an intrinsic value of only 50¢ or $1.00 trade in the thousands of dollars.

These high premiums, combined with relatively easy production, have created a flood of counterfeit coins in recent years. Establishing the true age of a coin is an extremely cumbersome, but necessary process. Be careful to select only a dealer whose reputation and integrity are beyond any doubt. Keep in mind that ancient coins have excessively high premiums and can be very hard to negotiate.

So far, we have concentrated on coins. But in the numismatic sector there is also the vast category of "medallions." Medallions are usually struck by governments, institutions or even private individuals, to commemorate an event. They are not legal tender (even if struck by governments) and therefore never show a face value. Medallions may have appeal to collectors but they make a risky and questionable investment.

Another area you should positively stay away from is that of "private issues." At one time or another, most of us have received brochures advertising the coins of private mints and refining institutions. Printed and distributed at very high cost, these offerings are directed at the "serious investor." The buyer of such issues usually pays a hefty premium for all the expenses of the mail order promotion. Premiums in this sector range from 40% to as much as 200% over actual gold content. A frequent approach is to term such selling campaigns as "limited issues"—the limit generally being the number of coins the promoter can sell.

A good way of protecting yourself against a bad investment is to stay away from private issues altogether. However, if an issue appeals to you personally, and you want to buy it, demand from the selling institution the exact details regarding fine gold content of the coins and compare its gold value to its price. Do not expect any dealer to pay a premium for the esthetic appeal of the coin (or metal)—the best you can usually expect to recoup from such items is the market value of the gold it contains.

Gold Mining Shares

The first thing you have to know about investing in gold mining shares is that you are not investing only in gold. To an equal degree you are investing in the future of a corporation, which makes the issue much more complicated. Instead of analyzing only the outlook for the gold price, which is difficult enough in itself, you also have to examine closely the corporate health of the specific mine you will be purchasing a share of.

Initially, you must familiarize yourself with the background of the corporation, its recent development and its prospects for future production. You should also look at a projection of earnings, the capitalization, the dividends, and other important statistical information. In addition, there are a number of factors which pertain specifically to mining stocks.

A very important consideration is how much it costs the mine to produce one ounce of gold. The production cost usually depends on the grade of the gold mined. In general, the lower the grade, the higher the production cost. Production cost and grade are therefore important investment considerations. You would hardly want to invest in a mine if the production cost were $290 per ounce of gold while the market price was $220. On the other hand, if the gold price reached $300, a mine with that production cost would suddenly have an excellent outlook.

Many smaller mines and mining properties, which are not now operative, may suddenly become profitable if gold prices continue to rise. Some of them will be run by their current owners and others will become candidates for takeover by larger corporations. There are a number of factors which affect the production cost. To name only some of them, there are labour costs, corporate management,

advantages:	Highly liquid.
	Prices are widely quoted.
	Dividends.
	Canadian citizens can defer income invested in Canadian mining corporations by placing shares into a Retirement Savings Plan.
disadvantages:	More knowledge required.
	You invest in more than just gold.
	Relatively expensive (high transaction charges).
	You are tied to "lots" (usually multiples of 100 shares), if you want to avoid even higher commission charges.
	Money tie-up.
opportunities and pitfalls:	Make sure your broker understands mining shares and the gold market.
	If you deal in foreign mining shares, choose a broker who specializes in them.
	Check taxation on foreign shares.
	Avoid investment in unlisted shares.

taxation changes, and the state of equipment to worry about. Another consideration in analyzing a mining operation is the "life" of a mine. The life is the time a mine can be expected to operate at unchanged production levels. In other words, the expected reserves of gold in the ground determine the mine's life. A mining operation with a very short life is obviously not suitable as a long-term investment.

You should bear in mind that the purchase and sale of mining shares, like other stock market transactions, are subject to a broker's commission of around 3%. On the other hand, the investor is normally paid dividends which should more than compensate.

As you can see, investing in mining stocks is not an easy proposition. The guidance of a good broker is absolutely essential unless you are an astute investor and are experienced in stock market transactions, in the basics of mining share analysis, and are familiar with the outlook for the gold bullion price. You will find that only very few brokers are familiar with the precious metals market and able to give you guidance as far as gold mining shares go. Some brokerage houses specialize in gold shares—those are the people you should contact.

On page 130, you will find a listing of all major Canadian, United States, and South African gold mining shares. The listings include the price range of each share during the first half of 1979, the life, the grade, and the approximate production cost per ounce of gold for each mining operation.

Penny Gold Stocks

Most of the "penny gold stocks" or "penny mining stocks" are stocks of companies which have not done any mining at all. There is a widespread misconception that penny stocks are the stocks of smaller mines. In reality, these stocks represent companies which have some property that may qualify for exploration or even mining at much higher gold prices. In other words, if penny stocks are what you are interested in, you must be ready to put your money into a company that has no proven reserve of gold ore, no record of past production, and usually very little money in the bank.

The idea behind most penny stocks is that sooner or later a considerable boom in gold mining will develop in North America. As gold climbed from below $100 per ounce to almost $300 per ounce, a small number of corporations owning potential mining properties performed well. With a much higher gold price, it was suddenly feasible to produce gold and some of these companies were taken over by large mining corporations. When that happened, the prices of such stocks went up 10 to 20 times.

On the other hand, it should be observed that the vast majority of such exploration properties are never taken over or developed. Those favoring penny stocks will argue that large-scale mining development will take place if the gold price goes up much further. Realistically, an investment in penny stocks has to be termed highly speculative. They are only suitable for the investor who wishes to put aside some portion of his investment capital to take risks with. Another factor to bear in mind is that there is no liquid market in these stocks and it is therefore hard to negotiate them.

If, after reading this, you still wish to invest in penny gold stocks, stick to the following guidelines:

advantages:	Speculative appeal.
disadvantages:	High risk. Low negotiability. Money tie-up. Expensive (usually high transaction costs). You do not invest in gold but in exploration. Price quotations are difficult to obtain.
opportunities and pitfalls:	Avoid companies with debt. Make sure the shares you purchase can be traded somewhere. If you invest several thousand dollars, do not purchase shares of only one company, but diversify. Do not purchase penny stocks unless you are prepared to lose it all.

1. Select shares of corporations which do not have any debt.

2. Corporations in this category are usually run by one or two people. Find out who they are and meet them. If possible, check out their background.

3. Contact your broker and get a market opinion on the stock. Usually, you won't find out much, but the broker's comments will likely remind you of the risk you are taking.

4. Have your broker confirm to you that there is an established market for the stock.

5. Do not put much money into any one of the penny stocks. If you must invest larger amounts, diversify it into the shares of five or ten different corporations. As a rule of thumb, do not put more than $1,000 into any one penny stock.

Gold Futures Contracts

The concept of a futures contract was initially designed to provide protection against ever-increasing fluctuations in the prices of commodities and foreign currencies. In the gold sector, the people seeking such protection are primarily industrial users. Let us assume that a jewelry manufacturing and wholesale operation wants to prepare its fall sales campaign. It is now mid-summer and during the past three months gold has been trading as low as $230 and as high as $285. Where the gold price will be in the fall is strictly a matter of speculation. At the same time, price lists and catalogues have to be prepared and they of course have to be based on a certain price level. Instead of leaving itself open to further

advantages:	You can also profit if the gold price goes down.
	Leverage: your money tie-up is substantially reduced.
	Liquidity.
	You invest only in gold.
	Futures contracts are widely quoted.
	Tax advantage: current tax legislation allows you to choose either income tax treatment or capital gains treatment, provided you are consistent.
	Speculative appeal.
	No storage risk.

disadvantages:	You can only deal in certain "contract sizes."
	You can only deal for delivery on a certain "contract date."
	You can only deal during set trading hours.
	If delivery is taken, you receive your gold in an exchange warehouse (Chicago, New York, or Winnipeg).
	Open risk: there is theoretically no limit to your loss.
	When actively trading futures, you are very dependent on your broker.
opportunities and pitfalls:	Trading in gold futures is a complex matter.
	Be absolutely certain your broker understands all the ins and outs of the futures market and passes them on to you. If in doubt, write for descriptive literature to:

International Monetary Market
West Jackson Blvd.
Chicago, Illinois, U.S.A. 60606

Commodity Exchange Inc.
4 World Trade Center
New York, New York, U.S.A. 10048

The Winnipeg Commodity Exchange
678–167 Lombard Avenue
Winnipeg, Manitoba R3B 0V7

fluctuations in the gold price, this company will typically purchase in the futures market the amount of gold it anticipates it will need in the fall.

How the Market Works

But you can also protect yourself by selling on the futures market. Take, for example, a typical mining company. Over the past two years, the company's management has watched the gold price climb ever higher and now wonders whether this trend can continue much longer. At the same time they know that between now and the end of the year they will produce a total of 28,000 ounces of gold. The company has met all its profit objectives and, if it sold its next six months' production at current prices, the company's performance would be improved further. Smart management will go out and sell 28,000 ounces of gold in the futures market.

Futures contracts are most commonly traded at commodity exchanges. The major exchanges are Chicago, New York, and Winnipeg and their function is to provide an organized mechanism for the buying and selling of contracts by the general public. The exchanges themselves do not directly purchase or sell futures contracts. They merely provide the facilities for their trading within established rules and regulations.

Today, gold futures contracts are no longer primarily used for their protective appeal to industrial users. In fact, the concept of the futures contract has attracted just the opposite sentiment: speculators are now the single largest group of users of this investment alternative. The main attraction to the speculator is leverage: the ability to put down a small deposit to guarantee the price of a large transaction.

Astonished by the staggering volume of business transacted in North American commodity exchanges (at times the volume in Chicago surpasses that of London and Zurich combined!), a European banker recently asked me how many private investors were really buying and selling futures contracts. When I told him that just about every one of my clients had at one time or another held gold futures contracts, he looked at me in disbelief. Coming from a culture where gold is purchased and then kept for twenty or thirty years, he simply could not understand why average investors would give themselves to this kind of speculation.

True, fortunes are made and lost every day in gold futures contracts. Always remember: for every buyer there is a seller; for every winner there is a loser. However, the futures market need not be only for speculators. To the astute investor, many of its characteristics prove highly useful and attractive. But it is absolutely essential that he knows his risk and understands the complexities governing this investment sector. If futures are what you are headed for, the following section, if read carefully, could save you thousands of dollars in a single year.

Let us examine how futures contracts work, how and when they are traded, and what possibilities there are to explore.

To every futures transaction, there are four parties involved. There is the customer, a broker, a floor broker, and the exchange staff. Just exactly how these people relate to each other is best illustrated in the chart you will find on page 99.

Let's assume you enter a futures transaction for 100 ounces of gold and your transaction date is next December 15. There are two possibilities: either you are a buyer of gold, or you are a seller.

If you have decided to purchase gold, you contact your broker and tell him you want to purchase ("go long") 100 ounces of gold (one contract) through the Chicago exchange, for delivery in December. The broker will call you back and confirm this transaction to you. Since you are not an industrial user, you probably have no intention of taking delivery of the gold in Chicago. You merely intend to sell the gold again ("liquidating the contract") at a higher price prior to December. The profit you hope to realize will be the difference between the price at which you purchased the gold and the price you set when you sell, minus commissions and other charges.

But what do you do if you think the price of gold is going to go down? Call your broker and tell him you want to sell ("go short," "sell short") 100 ounces of gold (one contract) through the Chicago market for December delivery. Your broker will again call you back with a confirmation. Once the transaction is confirmed, you have contractually promised to deliver 100 ounces of gold to Chicago no later than December. It is probably not your intention to deliver this gold because to begin with, you probably don't have it. The idea behind selling gold is to purchase it back at a lower price prior to December. If you do so, you don't actually have to deliver the gold. Yours has been purely a paper transaction. But the profits you have made, the difference between the price you sold gold at and the price you paid to repurchase it, are real.

In either case, you have made a promise to the exchange (via the broker), which has been matched by an opposite promise made by someone else (through his broker). Because you have contracted to deliver at a specified time in the future either gold (if you have sold), or money (if you have bought gold) worth approximately $30,000 (current value of a 100 ounce contract), the exchange makes sure they have some guarantee that you will indeed deliver. What they ask for is a "margin deposit." The exchanges set minimum deposits to which the brokerage industry must adhere. But individual brokers may increase these deposit sizes and in fact usually do. The current deposit required for a 100 ounce contract is around $2,000, or approximately six percent. This leverage factor is the single most important reason behind the success of futures contracts in North America. With as little as $2,000 down, you can purchase $30,000 worth of gold!

Your Risk

However, don't believe that this $2,000 is the extent of your risk. This is merely a deposit or a guarantee against your obligation. Within guidelines, the broker can at any time ask you for more. Should your investment start to lose money, he will "call margin" or "make a margin call." In other words, he will ask you to increase your margin deposit. Let us assume that you put down $2,000 against one contract. Since then the gold price has moved in the wrong direction and you are down $10 per ounce. On a 100 ounce contract this amounts to a loss of $1,000. You are still convinced that the gold price will turn around and start to move in your favour and therefore you do not want to liquidate the contract. Your broker, unfortunately, does not share your opinion. His only concern is the exchange regulation which dictates that he has to ask you for more money. Inevitably, he will ask you to make up the extent of your loss and deposit an additional $1,000.

Restrictions

The major disadvantage with commodity futures contracts is that they operate along certain set guidelines. For example, you cannot purchase seventy or eighty ounces of gold. It has to be a standard contract size. You cannot purchase or sell gold at 9:00 A.M. It has

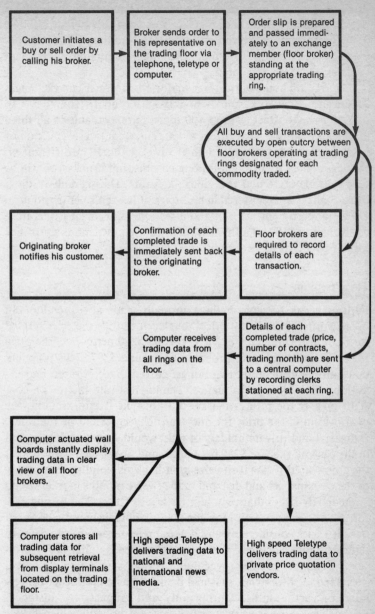

Customer initiates a buy or sell order by calling his broker.

Broker sends order to his representative on the trading floor via telephone, teletype or computer.

Order slip is prepared and passed immediately to an exchange member (floor broker) standing at the appropriate trading ring.

All buy and sell transactions are executed by open outcry between floor brokers operating at trading rings designated for each commodity traded.

Originating broker notifies his customer.

Confirmation of each completed trade is immediately sent back to the originating broker.

Floor brokers are required to record details of each transaction.

Computer receives trading data from all rings on the floor.

Details of each completed trade (price, number of contracts, trading month) are sent to a central computer by recording clerks stationed at each ring.

Computer actuated wall boards instantly display trading data in clear view of all floor brokers.

Computer stores all trading data for subsequent retrieval from display terminals located on the trading floor.

High speed Teletype delivers trading data to national and international news media.

High speed Teletype delivers trading data to private price quotation vendors.

Elements of a typical futures transaction

to be during exchange trading hours. You cannot simply ask your broker for a quotation and, if he gives you one, say "Okay, I'll take it." He can only quote you an indication. Trading in futures contracts, like trading in other exchange-dominated investment vehicles, is totally regulated.

The trading hours in the three major North American exchanges —Chicago, New York, and Winnipeg—are roughly from 9:30 A.M. to 2:30 P.M. Contract sizes of 100 ounces are available in all three markets; Winnipeg also offers a 400-ounce contract. You cannot trade for delivery just any month at any exchange. The different exchanges adhere to different trading months, but usually you will be able to trade up to two years into the future. During daily trading, price changes are registered in multiples of ten cents per troy ounce. On a standard contract of 100 ounces, one movement is therefore equivalent to $10 and a fluctuation of $1 is equivalent to a profit or loss of $100.

The Premium

Futures prices for gold bullion normally trade at a premium. In other words, if the "spot price" or "cash price" (the price quoted for bullion for immediate delivery) is u.s.$280 per ounce, the price for six-months gold will probably be around $297. This premium takes into consideration two things: current interest rates, and the outlook for gold's performance. The interest rate factor is a constant one. If the futures market did not take it into account, the cash price and the price for one-year delivery would be the same. Industrial and private holders of gold would simply sell their gold in the cash market for $280 per ounce, and invest their cash float at the going interest rate for twelve months. This simultaneous supply to the cash market and demand in the twelve months market would immediately bring that premium back into force. The second factor, that of the price outlook for gold, is obviously not a constant one. It varies considerably and makes premiums on future delivery dates for gold fluctuate. When the gold price is under heavy pressure, premiums contract; when gold is on a steady upward curve, they expand. Moreover, seasonal demand has an influence on certain contract months. During July and August, for instance, Europe's sizeable jewelry industry goes on holiday, which brings demand for gold down.

Market Orders

Let's say you like the three-month outlook and wish to purchase a contract. You have also looked at the premium and you can live with it. You now have to contact your broker. There are three ways in which you can place your order. You can place it "at market," in which case you agree to accept whatever price the contract is trading at when your transaction is executed on the trading floor of the exchange, or you can place the order at a certain price level. In other words you can "put the order in" at, for instance, U.S.$287, in which case your order only gets filled if that price is met. However, if between the placement of your order and the time it reaches the trading floor the market moves sufficiently to make your order impossible, your order may not "get filled." Similarly, the market may touch $287 but there may not be sufficient sellers to meet all buy orders and again your order may be the one that does not get executed. A specified order can be placed just for the day or you can make it an "open order," in which case it stands until it is revoked.

You can also place an M.I.T. order. M.I.T. stands for "Market If Touched," which is a combination between a market order and a specified order. M.I.T. is probably the best choice available. Open market orders are always dangerous while with specified orders there is the risk of not getting filled. M.I.T. orders allow the floor broker at the exchange to put in your order at market once a price level set by yourself is reached. If, for example, you place an order for purchase of one contract at $287 M.I.T., the order will be placed at market as soon as the market touches $287. If there are not enough sellers at $287, and the market moves to $287.10 or $287.20, your order will get filled then. Again, you can place M.I.T. orders just for the day or you can make them "open orders."

Limit Days

One feature only found in futures markets are 'limit days." During any one market day, prices fluctuations are limited to $10 per troy ounce above or below the closing date of the preceding trading day. When the price is "limit up," trading is suspended.

Limit days are something you should fully expect if you enter the futures market. They will put strains on your liquidity which you must anticipate. If you are on the wrong side of the market, a limit day will most certainly result in a telephone call from your broker, who will want more money. The next day, gold may be down further, and you may decide there is worse to come. You therefore tell the broker to liquidate your contract. It may well happen that by the time your order is in, the market is down limit again; trading has therefore been suspended and more money is due. The gold market has experienced three limit days in a row more than once before and it will undoubtedly happen again.

Stop Losses

One way to protect yourself against such limit down days is by putting in a "stop loss." This strategy allows you to place an open order to liquidate your contract at a certain price level. Let us say you have purchased one contract of gold at $287. While you think you should make money on this contract, you recognize that the gold market is a volatile one and that your investment may also go against you. Your decision is that a $500 loss is the maximum you wish to incur. When your broker confirms your purchase to you, you therefore put in an open order for sale of your contract at $282. If the market dips down two or three dollars, you won't be affected at all; if it continues to rise, you will make a profit, but if it drops $10 (a potential loss of $1,000) you will very likely only lose $500.

However, you should understand that placement of stop losses does not give you total protection. As you have seen above, an M.I.T. stop-loss order would give you more protection than a specific order, but neither of them is guaranteed. Because of the nature of an exchange system, there are times when markets slide and slide and there are just not enough buyers to absorb all the gold offered—precisely because it is going down. Another problem can arise when your stop-loss is placed between the close of one day and the opening of the next day. Let's look again at the gold contract you bought at $287 on which you have wisely placed a stop-loss at $282. A week later, the gold price drops from an opening of $293 to a "limit-close" of $283. After the bullion price is pushed down further overnight in the Far East and Europe, your contract opens next morning at $274. Are you safely out of gold? No.

To those using them as a speculative vehicle, futures contracts are just what they asked for: very risky. To the long-term investor, on the other hand, there need not be much risk at all.

Reduce Leverage — Reduce Risk

A tactic of many wealthy investors is to utilize all the advantages of the futures market while avoiding its risks. Instead of purchasing bullion they buy gold contracts through one of the exchanges and simply hold on to them. No stop-losses are placed, so the value of the gold can fluctuate as freely as if they held bullion in a safety deposit box with a bank. At the same time, they benefit from the availability of their money which, with a bullion investment, would have been tied up. Investors of this type will staunchly refuse to purchase in the futures market more gold than they would have bought elsewhere. They usually select the nearest available delivery date because the premium is the lowest. When the delivery date approaches, they simply liquidate their existing contract and purchase a new one. The advantages they gain from the investment of their money compensate for the high brokerage costs.

Those with a more active investment approach, wishing to trade their gold holdings, generally prefer delivery dates giving them some flexibility. In spite of the higher premium, they will often choose a date five or six months in the future. This is because they anticipate an event that will drive the gold price in their direction, but are not sure about the timing of the expected price correction. Distant delivery dates (over nine months) are primarily used by industrial users of gold bullion and by professional traders.

Comparison

There are those who can make a case for bullion and there are others who advise the purchase of gold futures contracts. Bullion offers you the security of holding the investment in your own hands. You can trade it during banking hours at any time, in any country, and through any bank or dealer. It is far less cumbersome as a long-term investment; you simply leave it in your bank safety deposit box or hold onto it yourself. On the other hand, you have some $60,000 tied up in this investment, which you could use elsewhere.

With a futures contract, you can take advantage of a gold price increase and continue to earn income on your money. Another big plus is that you can sell a futures contract and make money out of a downturn in the gold price.

On the negative side, there are a number of specific guidelines and trading regulations you will have to adhere to. Every time your contract matures you have to renew it, which is both a bother and costly. In addition, you don't hold the bullion but merely a broker's promise that someone else will deliver gold to you at a future date.

Trading in futures contracts has many advantages and disadvantages. My personal opinion is that the futures contract is not suitable as a long-term investment in gold, but presents excellent trading opportunities for those investors willing to learn its intricacies.

Call Options

If you have read the chapter on gold futures contracts, you already know the principles of leverage, which also apply to options. The main difference between a futures contract and an option is the following.

By purchasing a futures contract, you promise to purchase gold at a specified price at a specified date in the future. By purchasing an option, you do not promise to purchase but you do have the *right* to purchase gold at a specified price at a certain date in the future.

Since you have the right, but not the duty, to purchase the gold, an option provides you with a *defined risk*. The extent of your risk is neither more nor less than the cost of the option.

Quotations

The table on page 107 shows you a typical quotation sheet for gold options. On the left-hand side is a description of the unit size, which in our example is 100 ounces. Underneath, the current cash price for bullion is quoted at u.s.$280 per ounce. The next column contains a number of "striking prices," namely the prices at which you can buy or sell gold.

The primary factor in options markets are the "premiums" which are displayed in the following three columns. The premiums are the per-ounce prices at which options are traded at certain striking prices for certain maturity dates. When you purchase the right to buy gold, there is a price for that right and you have to "pay a premium." On the other hand, if you give someone else the right to buy your gold, you sell this right and you "receive a premium."

advantages:	Speculative appeal.
	Leverage: you reduce your money tie-up.
	Clearly defined risk.
	You invest only in gold.
	No storage risk.
disadvantages:	You can only deal along certain contract sizes, trading hours and maturity dates.
	Slightly more expensive than futures contracts.
	Less liquid and negotiable than futures contracts.
	If delivery is taken, you end up holding gold in New York, Winnipeg, or Geneva.
	Options prices are not yet widely quoted.
opportunities and pitfalls:	Gold options are a complex matter: make sure you fully understand them. If in doubt, write to: Valeurs White Weld S.A., 1 Quai du Mont-Blanc, 1211-Geneva, Switzerland, who publish an excellent free brochure entitled "Options on Gold Bullion". (Also available at the offices of Guardian Trust Company in Canada).
	A prospectus on options on gold futures contracts traded in Winnipeg is available through most brokerage houses.

Those dealers and exchanges providing a market for gold options act in the same capacity as the commodities exchanges do in the case of futures contracts. If you purchase an option, you have to buy it outright. Because you do not need to exercise your right to buy the gold when the maturity date arrives, the dealer or the exchange runs no risk. Your option has been paid for. On the other hand, when you sell an option you are giving someone else the right to buy gold from you and therefore there is a risk involved. After all, the dealer or the exchange does not know whether you actually possess the gold you have contracted to sell. They will not pay you the premium they receive from the buyer of the option until maturity date. Moreover, you may be asked to provide some security, either in the form of evidence that you hold gold, or in the form of a deposit.

Quotations for Gold Options

	Striking Price	31 Aug.	31 Oct.	31 Dec.
Gold Bullion Call Options for 100 ounce Units	270	10.30–11.30	16.50–17.50	21.50–22.50
	275	8.80– 9.80	14.50–15.50	19.50–20.50
	280	7.30– 8.30	13.00–14.00	18.00–19.00
	285	5.80– 6.80	11.50–12.50	15.50–17.50
	290	3.80– 3.80	9.00–10.00	13.00–14.00
Current Cash Price	U.S. $280/oz.			June 20/79.

Buying a Call Option . . .

Let us assume you want to purchase a call option ("buy an option") for 100 ounces of gold. The current cash price for bullion is $280 per ounce, and you are convinced that by the end of August, gold will be trading better than $290. Looking at the different striking prices available, you decide to go for $275 per ounce. According to the quotation sheet, you can pick up the option to buy at that price for a premium of $9.80 for a maturity date of August 31. In other words, for $980 (for 100 ounces) you buy the right to purchase gold at $275 per ounce on August 31. In order to break even, gold has to rise to at least $284.80 by maturity date. We have arrived at that figure by adding the striking price of $275 with the premium of $9.80. If the gold price goes up further than that, you will realize a profit. If, on the other hand, the gold price drops below $275, the most you can lose is $980, namely the price of your option.

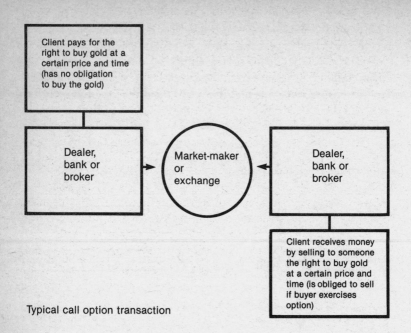

Client pays for the right to buy gold at a certain price and time (has no obligation to buy the gold)

Dealer, bank or broker

Market-maker or exchange

Dealer, bank or broker

Client receives money by selling to someone the right to buy gold at a certain price and time (is obliged to sell if buyer exercises option)

Typical call option transaction

. . . and Trading It

Options can be negotiated prior to maturity date. You do not have to wait until the option comes due and take delivery of the gold bullion. But watch out: if you trade before maturity date, you essentially trade the premium and not the gold bullion. Options trading is even more complicated than the trading of futures contracts, and they are not nearly as liquid and negotiable. The primary reason for this is that most markets provide a wide range of striking prices and maturity dates for a market which is significantly smaller than that for gold futures. Therefore, it can happen quite easily that a certain striking price and maturity date are simply "out of favor."

Another potential pitfall is the possibility that the bullion price will rise, while the premium (the price of your option) declines. This is because the closer you get to maturity date, the less attractive it becomes for others to buy your option. In mid-June, it is still quite possible that the gold price may experience sizeable fluctuations before a November maturity date. By mid-October, however, it is very unlikely that anything significant will happen and it is much simpler for an investor to just wait and buy in the cash market. However, if your premium has declined because the maturity date is near (and not because the gold price has dropped sharply) you will probably realize a nice profit by exercising your option. Take delivery of the gold and sell it at a profit.

As with futures contracts, leverage is the main attraction of gold options. It allows the investor to put elsewhere the major portion of what he would ordinarily have had to tie up in the purchase of gold.

For example, our investor has paid $980 for an option instead of the $28,000 he would have had to put down if he purchased the gold outright. Let's say he invests the balance of $27,020 in a 10% term deposit for the remaining 42 days (until maturity date). If he obtains a profit on his option, it will be compounded by the additional $300 he has earned in interest. If, in the worst case, he loses the entire value of his option, the interest generated on the balance reduces his loss by almost one-third.

Selling a Call Option

Now, suppose a long-term holder of bullion decides he wants to sell a call option ("write an option"). Let us say that our investor holds 100 ounces of gold at an average price of $280. Gold is now trading at $285 and he does not expect the price to go higher in the near term. He is actually concerned that gold may drop $10.00 or $20.00. To protect his investment, he could sell one option against the 100 ounces he holds. On our quotation table, we see that he can obtain $5.80 per ounce for an August 31 option at a striking price of $285. Accordingly, he would incur no loss in his bullion position until the market price reached $274.20 per ounce. We arrive at this figure by deducting from his average price of $280 the premium of $5.80 he will receive. On the other hand, he would not be asked to deliver his bullion if the price did not rise to above $285. If it did, he would sell at a $5.00 per ounce profit and he would still make an additional $5.80 per ounce from the premium he would collect. In addition to these alternatives, the investor is free to trade his option before maturity date if he sees a particularly good opportunity.

Although protecting yourself by the purchase or sale of an option is generally more expensive than the equivalent transaction in the futures market, it is a price investors are increasingly willing to pay. They gain excellent investment flexibility and a clearly defined risk.

Market Makers

In the United States, the market for call options is made by Mocatta Metals Corporation of New York, who feature a wide range of striking prices and maturity dates. Options are for 100-ounce units. Mocatta is also active in call options for South African Krugerrands. Trading is in units of 100 pieces.

Europe's largest dealer in options on gold bullion is Valeurs White Weld S.A. of Geneva, a wholly owned subsidiary of Credit Suisse First Boston. Valeurs White Weld options provide excellent liquidity and, in my opinion, are consistently quoted with a very reasonable difference between the buying and selling premiums. A slight disadvantage to North American investors is that these Swiss options are denominated in five-kilogram units (equivalent to 160.75 troy ounces). However, striking price and premiums are quoted on a U.S. dollar per ounce basis to facilitate trading. For those who have access to a Reuters monitoring system, Valeurs White Weld transmits dealing quotes continuously under code "vwww." Valeurs White Weld also publishes an excellent booklet called "Options on Gold Bullion," which is available free of charge. (See page 106.)

The Winnipeg Commodity Exchange recently introduced a concept which will make options trading even more flexible. Winnipeg options are not options on gold bullion, but options on gold futures contracts. These options are designed to tie in with the Winnipeg-traded gold futures contracts and are therefore denominated in 100-ounce units which mature in line with their futures contract delivery dates. This means you can protect yourself against transactions you have entered into in the futures market. Here's how:

Imagine that you have sold one contract of gold bullion on the futures market for the month of August. For some reason, you are worried about an increase in the price of gold. In that case, purchasing an option would establish the maximum price you would have to pay for the bullion in order to satisfy your obligations under the contract. In other words, if your futures contract went against you, you could take delivery of the gold you purchased on option and use it to close out the deal. In practice, the transaction is even simpler, because all you need to do is inform your broker to apply your option purchase against your futures contract sale. This is also an excellent example of how selecting a dealer with a wide range of services can be a definite advantage.

Call Options and Futures Contracts

Of course, similar protection could be obtained more cheaply by ordering a "stop-loss" against your open futures contract. But, as we have seen in our chapter on futures contracts, this is not an entirely foolproof alternative. Placing an option as a protection against a futures contract has more than just one advantage. If things do go against you and your stop-loss is executed you are no longer in the market. Not so with an option. Your futures contract and your option continue to ride until maturity date, which can be very important. After all, the gold price may go against you only temporarily and then forcefully correct into what, to you, is a profit position. If that happens, the profit from your futures contract will likely be significantly larger than the premium you paid for your call option.

Jewelry

"If things get really rough, I can always trade in my wife's jewelry" is a sentence that best illustrates the widespread belief that jewelry is a safe investment.

While gold jewelry offers classic appeal that makes it an incomparable gift, it cannot seriously be recommended as a good investment. For one thing, it is always dangerous to mix emotions with investments and it is seldom that I have met holders of jewelry who were not emotionally attached to their treasures. But there are a whole string of other factors that make jewelry an inferior investment in the gold sector.

To begin with, buyers of jewelry do not get the same quality of gold they would get if they purchased bullion. Gold is a relatively soft metal and therefore not suitable for use as jewelry in its pure form. It is usually alloyed down to standard finenesses of 22, 18, 14, 12 and even 10 karat. The 14-karat norm is by far the most

advantages:	Esthetic appeal.
disadvantages:	High cost. Low liquidity. Not easily negotiable. Not a direct investment in gold. Sales tax in most states and provinces.
opportunities and pitfalls:	If you want to combine the esthetic appeal of jewelry with a direct gold investment, purchase a framed ingot.

popular. Once the craftsman takes delivery of the gold in its now alloyed form, he usually puts considerable workmanship and expertise into the finished piece of jewelry he makes. Furthermore, on the way from his workshop to the store shelf, jewelry is heavily taxed and an array of production, wholesale and retail markups are added to the base price. Not only is it very unlikely that you will be able to recover these additional costs but, in a crisis, you may even have to pay refining costs when you try to sell.

In this connection, I am again reminded of the plight of those Vietnamese refugees who came to the U.S. While most brought gold wafers with them, some carried jewelry. Those carrying bullion had to pay refining charges because their wafers were made by unknown foreign producers. However, the three or four percent charge was a small price to pay for the convenience of being able to instantly acquire local purchasing power.

Now here's what happened to those refugees carrying gold jewelry. They received the equivalent of the gold value of their jewelry after refining charges had been deducted. But they lost everything they had paid for in the production of the jewelry, the taxes applied to it, and the selling markups. In most cases, they had lost the major portion of their original investment.

Always remember, it is estimated that one dollar's worth of gold has been converted into a $6.50 price tag by the time you buy the finished product.

In ancient times, gold jewelry was so treasured it was only available to emperors and kings — an appeal that gold maintains to this day. In the Middle Ages, the goldsmith was the most highly honored of all artisans. Today, most citizens of the industrially developed world will at one time or another own gold jewelry. The esthetic appeal of gold jewelry is unsurpassed but it lacks the factors which would make it a worthwhile investment.

---

fact:

In 1967 the U.S. Federal Trade Commission defined "solid gold" as "any article that does not have a hollow centre and has a fineness of ten karat or higher.". . . Investors beware!

Gold Funds

A variety of dealers and brokers offer their own gold funds. All incoming investment money is pooled and investors then own a percentage of the whole in accordance with the size of their investment.

Most funds specializing in the gold sector are now based in the United States, although McEwen Easson of Toronto also offers a gold fund. Funds vary in their strategy from investing strictly in gold bullion to investments in a variety of vehicles. Most funds tend to concentrate heavily on mining shares.

The basic advantage of a managed fund is that it allows you to purchase a professional manager's expertise. You pay for this service in the form of a fee which is usually charged to the fund.

Bear in mind that you can participate with a relatively modest amount of money. This, in many cases, is offset by the fact that on small amounts you will have to pay heavy commissions when purchasing units — usually between five and ten percent! And, while a few funds have shown excellent results over the years, the performance of most has been poor.

It is difficult to give specific advice regarding investment in gold funds mainly because there is such a variety of them, each one specializing in a different concept. However, I would recommend that you contact your broker and obtain a prospectus before you commit yourself to the purchase of units in any particular fund. Pay special attention to the section dealing with selling commissions and management fees. Ask your broker about the performance of the fund you are interested in and familiarize yourself with the strategy and objectives the managers use in its running.

Managed Investment Accounts

Although "portfolio accounts" or "managed accounts" are becoming more popular in Europe and the United States, few Canadian dealers offer them. The advantage to the investor is the fact that he does not have to pay a heavy selling commission to his broker. Instead, the client pays a standard management fee and any normal banking charges the dealer incurs on his behalf. In some cases, a special "performance fee" is also payable. This is designed to give the dealer an incentive to make the most out of your dollars.

Because dealers offering this service give away a considerable amount of expertise for a relatively small fee, they can usually afford to be picky. Most dealers want to know just as much about their clients as their clients do about them. Some insist on lengthy interviews with prospective investors during which they endeavour to ensure that the investor understands clearly what is involved in the dealer's investment strategy. At the same time, the dealer needs to know that his investment strategy indeed fits in with the investor's overall financial situation. Few dealers will accept investment amounts below $50,000. The norm is more like $100,000.

The first thing you have to realize about managed investment programs is that they are discretionary. In other words, you have absolutely no control over the manager's investment decisions; you have to give him full powers to dispose of your money as he sees fit. You also agree not to hold the dealer responsible if he happens to make a mistake and your money is lost.

Given that your financial holdings are relatively large, managed investment programs are often an excellent option. If you are a professional in your own field, and you have neither the time nor

115

the expertise to follow developments in the gold markets, a managed account is just what the doctor ordered. Most dealers devote considerable time to such investments because it is in their interest to impress their client and get a larger share of his business. At the same time, the price is right.

The decision as to which particular investment program you should choose depends on your views. Some bullion dealers offer fairly aggressive and active investment programs, while the approach of others is more long-term. Your best bet is to contact two or three dealers who offer such services and compare.

3

Directories
and Indices

Gold Talk . . .
a Guide to the Terminology

Acid Test

The fineness of gold can be determined by exposing the metal to various acids: higher quality gold can usually be tested by exposure to *aqua regia*, a combination of nitric and hydrochloric acids.

Alloy

A mixture of metals: gold is often alloyed with copper, nickel, silver or zinc to improve its hardness or to change its colour.

Arbitrage

To simultaneously buy and sell a commodity or security in different markets. An "arbitrageur" makes money by purchasing gold in Chicago and selling it at the same time in Winnipeg, taking advantage of a price differential. Such differences in the market price are usually so small that arbitrage trading requires substantial amounts to generate a profit.

The term arbitrage is also used for a whole string of complicated trading manoeuvres, exploiting differences in spot prices, futures prices and interest rates.

Assay, Assayer

An assay is a test of a metal in which its

purity is determined; an assayer has the function of conducting this analysis and usually confirms it by marking the gold accordingly.

Au

Chemical symbol for gold (*aurum*, Latin for gold).

Bullion

Gold in negotiable form; in most market places a purity of .995 or finer is required. Gold bullion is produced in the form of bars, wafers or ingots.

Cash Price

Also "spot price." The price required for immediate settlement. In gold markets, most transactions are cash transactions. The seller of gold therefore has to deliver the metal immediately (usually two business days) while the buyer has to pay for the gold in full at the same time. The term "cash" or "spot" is used to differentiate from a "futures transaction," where settlement is due at a time in the future.

Coin Gold

An alloy generally used for the production of gold coinage. In order to improve the durability, gold is usually mixed with silver and copper. Many European coins have a fineness of .75 (18 k), while in the u.s. a fineness of .90 (21.6 k) is used.

Discount

Mostly used in futures trading. A commodity may trade "at a discount" for delivery at a future time. This means that its price is quoted lower than if you were to purchase it today.

Ductility

Gold is the most ductile of all metals:

one single ounce of the metal can be drawn into a thin wire fifty miles long.

Electrolytic Gold

A refining process utilizing an electric current is applied to produce extremely high quality gold of .9999 purity.

Electroplating

An electric current is used to coat an item with a thin layer of gold.

Fine Gold

(Also pure gold). Chemical element with the symbol Au, a melting point of 1063° Celsius or 1945° Fahrenheit, a specific weight of 19.3 and an atomic weight of 197.2.

Fineness

Usually expressed in fine (pure) gold parts contained in 1000 parts of an alloy: a bar of a fineness of .995 (pronounced "two nines five") contains 995 parts of pure gold and five parts of another metal. Fineness is also expressed in karats, especially in the jewelry trade. The fineness is usually stamped onto gold—in "European Marking" in the case of bullion or jewelry manufactured on the continent, in "American Marking" when jewelry items made in North America are concerned.

The Fineness of Gold: in percentage	European Marking	American Marking
100%	.999	24 k
99 1/2%	.995	23.88 k
75%	.750	18 k
58 1/2%	.585	14 k

Fine Weight

The weight of pure gold contained in a bar or coin.

Fixings	The gold price is "fixed" twice a day in the London market. The five market participants (Johnson Matthey Bankers Ltd., Mocatta & Goldsmid Ltd, Samuel Montagu & Co. Limited, N. M. Rothschild & Sons Ltd. and Sharps Pixley Ltd.) meet and agree on a price at which they can settle transactions among themselves.
Flat	"Flattening out a position," "being flat," "a flat position" refer to a trader's net position in a commodity or security, meaning that his books show no holdings or liabilities. The term is used mostly in futures markets. For instance, if a trader has a flat gold position, his books show no "long positions" or "short positions" in the metal.
Fool's Gold	Iron pyrite is often mistaken for gold. The qualities of gold and iron pyrite are quite different: real gold is soft and malleable, the false version is hard and brittle.
"Four Nines"	The finest gold bullion or gold coinage available is gold with a fineness of .9999, or as the experts call it, "four nines fine gold."
Futures Contract	A contract between a buyer and seller of a commodity or security, setting its price and the date of delivery. If you purchase gold in the futures market, you undertake to pay a certain amount of money for it at an agreed date in the future.
Gilding	A gilded surface is a surface coated with a thin layer of gold. Today most sur-

faces are electroplated (see Electro-plating).

Gold Leaf

Gold hammered to extremely thin consistency. Gold leaf is used for a variety of purposes, most of which are decorative. Picture frames and book edges are the most common applications of gold leaf. The art of producing gold leaf dates back to ancient Egyptian times.

Gold Standard

A monetary system based on convertibility into gold, e.g. a nation issues paper currency and fully backs it with gold. The two "moneys," gold and paper, are freely interchangeable in terms of each other under a gold standard.

Grain

Originally the equivalent of one grain of wheat or barley, the grain is the earliest weight unit for gold. The "grain" is actually still used in the Avoirdupois System and in the Troy System. One grain is equivalent to 0.0648 grams, 24 grains make one pennyweight (dwt.) and one pound troy consists of 5,769 grains.

Gram

1/1000 of one kilogram. The continental European gold market is dominated by metric weights (kilograms, grams); the British market (U.K. and colonies) by troy ounces.

1 gram = 15.43 grains = 0.032 ounces troy

1 pound troy = 373.2 grams

32.15 ounces troy = 1,000 grams = 1 kilogram

Hallmark

A mark or a number of marks, which indicate the producer of a bar and its particulars (number, fineness, etc.).

Originally the hallmark was applied in England, where it was used as early as A.D. 1300. The goldsmiths used as many as six marks, showing quality, place of manufacture, a date letter and the producer.

Karat

Unit of fineness equal to $1/24$ part of pure gold in an alloy. The finest gold is 24 k.

Karat Gold

A gold of not less than 10 k. fineness.

Leverage

The ability to make an investment without committing its nominal value. If, for instance, you purchase 100 ounces of gold in the futures market, you only need to deposit around 10% of the total value. The rest of your money can be put to use elsewhere.

Limit Down
Limit Up

Trading in futures contracts is governed by certain limits set by the exchange. The 100 ounce gold contract, for instance, cannot move more than $10 per ounce in either direction in one trading day.

Liquid Gold

Usually used for surface decoration such as glass. A solution of gold (normally 12%) and a mixture of chemicals is painted on and then heated to a temperature of 540° Celsius. The resulting coating is only 0.1 microns thick (0.00004 inches).

Liquid gold is what you see as a coating on the windows of some modern buildings.

London Delivery Bar

Trading unit used in the London Gold Market. A London Delivery Bar (also "standard bar") is a bar weighing approximately 400 ounces troy, has a minimum fineness of .995 and carries the markings of a melter or assayer listed on the "good delivery list," a record of those refiners and assayers whose markings are internationally recognized.

London Market

The London Gold Market was the leading gold centre for centuries and remains one of the world's most important trading centres. The market is organized in terms of the trading hours and the specifications relating to trading units, quality, delivery, insurance and other aspects concerned. The London Gold Market also conducts two daily "gold fixings," which define the price of the yellow metal in U.S. dollar terms and which are reported around the world. The participants of the London market are:

Johnson Matthey Bankers Ltd.
Mocatta & Goldsmid Ltd.
Samuel Montagu & Co. Ltd.
N. M. Rothschild & Sons Ltd.
Sharps Pixley Ltd.

Long

"Going long" or "long position" describes the purchase of a commodity or security. Usually, the term is used for futures market transactions. To "go long gold" means to purchase gold in the hope of a price increase.

Malleability

Some metals can be extended considerably by hammering and do not crack or break in the process. Gold is the most malleable metal. It can be hammered to a thickness of only 0.000005 inches. One ounce of gold, in fact, can be beaten into a sheet covering over 100 square feet.

Marks

The stamp or stamps attached to each bar by its producers or by assayers. Producers usually mark a bar with its fineness, its weight, a bar number, their logo and the word "gold" or "fine gold." An assayer, testing only the fineness of a bar, will either stamp his logo under the fineness stamp of the original producer or will stamp on the fineness again.

Melter

Also referred to as the refiner, the melter is the producer of gold bullion. Buying gold from the mines, most melters refine the metal to a purity sufficient for acceptance in the world's gold markets and mark it accordingly.

Nugget

Gold washed from the rock and usually deposited in riverbeds. Nuggets are normally small in weight, although history reports some considerable findings. The largest nugget on record is one found in Australia in 1872, weighing almost 3,000 ounces troy (200 lbs.)

Option

The right to purchase or sell a commodity or security at a specified time in the future. You usually acquire this right at a certain price or are paid a certain price for it.

Pennyweight

Used in the United States as a unit of weight for gold. In Troy weight, twenty pennyweights equal one ounce. The term pennyweight dates back to England where, in the 17th century, it referred to the weight of one silver penny or $1/24$th of a Tower Pound.

Premium

Expression used for gold coinage. The premium is the amount by which the selling price of a coin exceeds the value of its fine gold content.

The expression "premium" is also used to express the difference between the "cash price" and the "future price" of a commodity or security. If gold for delivery in the future trades higher than the current gold price, gold is "at a premium."

Restrike

A coin made by the government that originally produced it, using the original die. Restrikes are also referred to as "new mintings."

Short

"Going short," "selling short," "having a short position" describe sales of a commodity or security you do not possess. Usually, the term is used in futures market transactions. To be short gold means that you have sold gold (which you did not own), hoping for a price decline.

Solid Gold

Surprisingly, the U.S. Federal Trade Commission allocated this term in a 1967 ruling to "any article that does not have a hollow center and has a fineness of ten karat or higher." Investors, beware of the term "solid gold."

Spot Price

See "cash price."

Spread

The difference between the buying and selling price. If gold is bought at $280 and sold at $282, the spread is two dollars. The term "spread" is used differently by futures contracts traders. See Straddle.

Standard Bar

See London Delivery Bar.

Stop Loss

The placement of a buying order or selling order against an existing futures contract. A stop loss is designed to limit potential loss. After buying a gold contract of 100 ounces at $280, you may decide the maximum loss you want to incur is $1,000. You therefore place a stop loss at $270, meaning your broker will automatically sell your contract if that price is reached.

Straddle

Used mostly in futures trading. A trader may find it advantageous to sell July gold and purchase simultaneously an identical amount of November gold, exploiting the price differential. Traders call this manoeuvre a "straddle" or a "spread."

Striking Price

Used mainly in options trading. The striking price is the price at which a commodity or security will change hands if an option is exercised.

Tael

Chinese gold weight; 1 tael = 1.2034 ounces troy of .9999 fineness.

Taels were almost totally restricted to Far Eastern markets until the end of the Vietnam War when thousands of refugees brought them to North America and Europe.

Taels come in the form of thin gold wafers (two and a half wafers make one tael), in the form of a coin with a round hole or in a shoelike shape. Far Eastern gold has recently been of very good quality.

The majority of the gold brought from the Far East was manufactured in Hong Kong, Saigon, Hanoi and Phnom Penh. Most items are stamped by "King Fook," "Lee Cheong" and "Kim Thanh."

Tola

Old gold weight. One tola equals 3.750 ounces or 111 grams, of .9999 fineness.

Troy Ounce

A unit of the troy system of weight used for the measurement of precious metals. Gold, silver, platinum and palladium are expressed in troy ounces.

1 troy ounce = 1.09711 ounces or 31.103 grams.

Wafer

Expression used for bullion manufactured in thin form ("gold wafer").

Year Mark

A letter symbol stamped onto gold by British goldsmiths. Each year has a different mark.

Guide to Major Gold Mining Operations*

The following list provides, in order: the name of the mine; the recent price range of its stock; an estimate of the mine's life; the grade of ore it produces; and the approximate production cost per ounce in 1978.

Canadian Mining Shares

Agnico-Eagle Mines Limited
$5³/₄—$8¹/₄
Long life
Medium grade
$100.00

Camflo Mines Limited
$12³/₄—$16¹/₈
Medium life
Medium grade
$70.00

Campbell Red Lake Mines Limited
$17³/₈—$24
Very long life
High grade
$50.00

Dickenson Mines Limited
$6¹/₄—$9¹/₈
Medium life
High grade
$135.00

Dome Mines Limited
$29⁵/₈—$48³/₄
Long life
Medium grade
$115.00

East Malartic Mines Limited
$130—$238
Long life
Low grade
$145.00

---

* Research information based on information made available by John Crowley, Analyst, James Sinclair & Company, New York and on quotations printed in The Northern Miner, Toronto. All price ranges quoted reflect the period from January to mid-June of 1979 in U.S. dollars.

Giant Yellowknife Mines
Limited
$10—$13$\frac{1}{2}$
Short life
High grade
$120.00

Kerr Addison Mines Limited
8\frac{7}{8}$—$13$\frac{3}{8}$
Short life
Medium grade
$120.00

Northair Mines Limited
$285—$485
Medium life
Medium grade
$110.00

Pamour Porcupine Mines Limited
5\frac{3}{4}$—$7$\frac{3}{4}$
Long life
Low grade
$160.00

Sigma Mines (Quebec) Limited
17\frac{7}{8}$—$27$\frac{1}{2}$
Long life
Low grade
$120.00

Willroy Mines Limited
$235—$325
Short life
Medium grade
$136.00

U.S. Mining Shares

Homestake Mining Company
31\frac{3}{4}$—$34$\frac{7}{9}$
Long life*
Low grade

Rosario Resources Corporation
$15—$27$\frac{1}{2}$

South African Mining Shares

Blyvooruitzicht
3\frac{3}{4}$—$7$\frac{1}{4}$
Short-Medium life
Medium grade
$107.00

Bracken
$0.85—$1.65
Short life
Medium grade
$91.00

Buffelsfontein
10\frac{1}{8}$—$16$\frac{7}{8}$
Long life
Medium grade
$119.00

Deelkraal
$1.25—$3.44
Long life
Medium grade

---

* Homestake has reserves of 14.9 million tons of gold ore, and the company accounts for 30% of total U.S. gold production. Gold output is not steady, but usually depends on prices. Other Homestake operations include uranium, lead, zinc, and silver mining, and forest products operations.

Doornfontein
$2^{7}/_{8}$—$7^{1}/_{4}$
Medium life
Medium grade
$122.00

Durban Roodepoort Deep
$3^{1}/_{2}$—$10^{1}/_{8}$
Short-Medium life
Low grade
$207.00

East Driefontein
$8^{3}/_{8}$—$15^{1}/_{8}$
Long life
High grade
$43.00

East Rand Proprietary Mines
$3.55—$9.65
Short life
Medium grade
$207.00

Eastern Transvaal
Consolidated Mines
$—
Medium life
Medium grade
$105.00

Elandsrand
$3.07—$7.25
Long life
Medium grade

Free State Geduld
$18^{1}/_{4}$—$26^{1}/_{8}$
Medium-Long life
$75.00

Ergo
$3.65—$4.90
Long life
Low grade

Free State Saaiplaas
$—
Medium life
Low grade
$218.00

Grootvlei
$1.22—$3.25
Short-Medium life
Low grade
$119.00

Harmony
$—
Medium life
Low-Medium grade
N/A

Hartebeestfontein
$14^{7}/_{8}$—$34^{7}/_{8}$
Medium life
Medium grade
$109.00

Kinross
$3^{1}/_{8}$—$6^{1}/_{4}$
Medium life
Medium grade
$87.00

Kloof
$6^{3}/_{8}$—$14^{1}/_{8}$
Long life
Medium-High grade
$90.00

132

Leslie
$0.74—$1.33
Short life
Low grade
$150.00

Libanon
$5³/₄—$13¹/₈
Medium life
Medium grade
$101.00

Loraine
$0.77—$2.00
Short-Medium life
Medium grade
$208.00

Marievale
$0.92—$2.45
Short life
Low grade
$102.00

President Brand
$10³/₈—$17³/₈
Medium life
Medium grade
$87.00

President Steyn
$8¹/₄—$15³/₄
Medium life
Medium grade
$123.00

Randfontein
$36¹/₂—$56
Long life
High grade
$59.00

St. Helena
$10—$16⁷/₈
Medium life
$87.00

S A Lands
$0.88—$2.09
Nil life
Low-Medium grade

South Roodepoort
$—
Short life
Low-Medium grade
$205.00

Southvaal
$5³/₄—$11³/₄
Medium life
Medium grade
$107.00

Stilfontein
$3⁷/₈—$7³/₄
Short-Medium life
Medium grade
$163.00

Unisel
$2.75—$5.40
Medium life
High grade

Vaal Reefs
$18—$33¹/₈
Medium-Long life
Medium grade
$116.00

Venterspost
$1^3/_4$—$5^1/_8$
Short-Medium life
Medium grade
$200.00

Vlakfontein
$0.55—$1.45
Short life
Low grade
$133.00

Welkom
$3^1/_8$—$5^3/_4$
Short-Medium life
Medium grade
$137.00

West Driefontein
$26^1/_4$—$49
Medium life
High grade
$48.00

West Rand Consolidated
$1.40—$3.17
Short-Medium life
Low grade
N/A

Western areas
$1^1/_2$—$3^1/_4$
Medium-Long life
Medium grade
$152.00

Western Deep Levels
$10—$16^3/_8$
Long life
High grade
$82.00

Western Holdings
$21^3/_4$—$36^1/_8$
Medium life
Medium grade
$80.00

Winkelhaak
$8^1/_8$—$14^1/_8$
Medium life
Medium grade
$75.00

Witwatersrand Nigel
$0.45—$1.10
Uncertain life
Low-Medium grade

Major Bullion Dealers

Canada

Bank of Nova Scotia
44 King Street West
Toronto, Ontario

Canadian Imperial Bank
of Commerce
Commerce Court West
Toronto, Ontario

Guardian Trust Company
618 St. James Street
Montreal, Quebec

Guardian Trust Company
87 Yonge Street
Toronto, Ontario

Great Britain

Johnson Matthey Bankers Ltd.
15 King Street
London

Mocatta & Goldsmid Ltd.
Park House
16 Finsbury Circus
London

Samuel Montagu & Co. Ltd.
114 Old Broad Street
London

N. M. Rothschild & Sons Ltd.
New Court
St. Swithin's Lane
London

Sharps Pixley Ltd.
34 Lime Street
London

Hong Kong

Hang Seng Bank Limited
77 Des Voeux Road Central
Hong Kong

Kleinwort Benson Limited
American International Tower
16–18 Queen's Road Central
Hong Kong

Mocatta Hong Kong Limited
902 Chartered Bank Building
4–4a Des Voeux Road Central
Hong Kong

N. M. Rothschild & Sons
(Hong Kong) Ltd.
1170/12 Connaught Centre
Hong Kong

Sharps Pixley Wardley Limited
Hutchison House, 5th floor
Harcourt Road
Hong Kong

Switzerland

Bank Julius Bär & Co. AG
Bahnhofstrasse 36
8022 Zurich

Bank Leu
Bahnhofstrasse 32
8022 Zurich

Credit Suisse
Paradeplatz
8021 Zurich

Swiss Bank Corporation
Paradeplatz
8021 Zurich

Union Bank of Switzerland
Bahnhofstrasse 45
8021 Zurich

Valeurs White Weld S.A.
1, quai du Mont-Blanc
1211 Geneve

Wozchod Handelsbank A.G.
Schützengasse 1
8023 Zurich

United States

J. Aron & Co. Inc.
160 Water Street
New York

Engelhard Minerals &
Chemicals Corp.
Philipp Brothers Division
1221 Avenue of the Americas
New York

Manfra Tordella & Brookes Inc.
59 West 49th Street
Rockefeller Center
New York

Mocatta Metals Corporation
25 Broad Street
New York

NMR Metals Incorporated
Suite 1012
1 Rockefeller Plaza
New York

Republic National Bank of
New York
452 Fifth Avenue
New York

Swiss Bank Corporation
Four World Trade Center
New York

West Germany

Commerzbank A.G.
32–36 Neue Mainzerstrasse
6000 Frankfurt/Main

Deutsche Bank A.G.
18 Rossmarkt
6000 Frankfurt / Main

DG Bank Deutsche
   Genossenschaftsbank

Wiesenthüttenstrasse 10
6000 Frankfurt / Main

Dresdner Bank A.G.
Gallusanlage 7–8
6000 Frankfurt / Main

Acceptable Refiners

Gold bullion manufactured by these refiners is recognized in most free gold markets.

Australia

Matthey Garrett Pty. Limited
Engelhard Industries Pty. Ltd.
The Perth Mint
Royal Mint

Belgium

Metallurgie Hoboken S.A.
Johnson, Matthey &
Pauwels S.A.

Canada

Canadian Copper Refiners Ltd.
Engelhard Industries of
   Canada Ltd.
Johnson Matthey Limited
Royal Canadian Mint

China

Refinery of China

France

Caplain-Saint-Andre
Compagnie des Metaux Precieux
Comptoir Lyon-Alemand,
   Louyot & Cie.
Laboratoires Boudet & Dussaix
Etablissements Leon Martin
Administration des Monnaies
   & Medailles

Great Britain

Johnson Matthey Chemicals
   Limited
Sheffield Smelting Co., Ltd.
N. M. Rothschild & Sons Ltd.[*]
Engelhard Industries Ltd.

* These names represent dealers who have bullion carrying their name manufactured through a refiner. Their products are internationally recognized.

Italy

Metalli Preziosi S.p.A.

Netherlands

H. Drijfhout & Zoon's
   Edelmetaalbedrijven NV
Schone's Essaier-Inrichting en
   Handel in Edele Metalen NV

Romania

Uzinele metalurgice de metale
   neferoase

South Africa

Rand Refinery Limited

Sweden

Swedish Mint

Switzerland

Metaux Precieux S.A.

Usine Genevoise de
   Degrossissage d'Or
Swiss Federal Mint /
   Monnaie Federale Suisse
Valcambi S.A.
Argor S.A.
Credit Suisse*
Swiss Bank Corporation*

U.S.A.

United States Assay Offices
United States Mints
American Smelting & Refining
   Company
Homestake Mining Company

U.S.S.R.

All Union Gold Factory
Soviet State Refinery

West Germany

Degussa / Deutsche Gold- und
   Silber-Scheideanstalt
W. C. Heraeus G.m.b.H.
Norddeutsche Affinerie (N.A.)

* These names represent dealers who have bullion carrying their name manufactured through a refiner. Their products are internationally recognized.

Acceptable Assayers

The following institutions are not in the refining business, but merely assay gold bullion. Their stamp or mark may therefore appear on bullion alongside the refiner's mark.

Great Britain

Daniel C. Griffith & Co. Ltd.

Romania

National Bank of the Socialist
  Republic of Romania

Switzerland

Bureau Central Suisse/Controle
  Metaux Precieux

Former Refiners

Although these institutions no longer manufacture bullion, their products are still in circulation. They are accepted by most international dealers.

Australia

The Royal Mint—Australian Branches
Garrett, Davidson & Matthey Pty., Limited

France

Jean Boudet
Fils de Paul Dubois / Robert Dubois
Comptoir Lyon-Alemand
Comptoir Lyon-Alemand et Marret, Bonnin,
  Lebel et Guieu reunis
Les Anciens Etablissements Leon Martin
Monnaie de Paris (French Mint)
Marret, Bonnin, Lebel et Guieu

Great Britain

Bank of England
F. Claudet Ltd.
Johnson & Sons, Assayers, Limited
Johnson Matthey & Co. Limited
Johnson & Sons Smelting Works Limited
H. L. Raphael's Refinery
Royal Mint

Netherlands

Rijks Munt (Dutch Mint)

South Africa

South African Mint

Books on Gold

Bayer, E. *Gold from the Oceans.* Extensive article in *Chemistry,* vol. 37, no. 10 (Oct. 1964).

Berton, Pierre. *The Golden Trail: the Story of the Klondike Rush.* Toronto: Macmillan of Canada, 1974.

Bresciani-Turroni, Costantino. *The Economics of Inflation: a Study of Currency Depreciation in Post-war Germany.* Translated by Millicent E. Savers. New York: A.M. Kelley, 1968.

Busschau, W.J. *Gold and International Liquidity.* Johannesburg: South African Institute of International Affairs, 1961.

Cartwright, Alan P. *Gold Paved the Way: the Story of the Gold-fields Group of Companies.* London: Macmillan, 1967.

Cassell, Francis. *Gold or Credit? The Economics and Politics of International Money.* New York: Praeger, 1965.

Charter Consolidated. Economic Intelligence Unit. *Gold: a World-wide Survey.* London, 1969.

Einzig, Paul. *The Destiny of Gold.* London: Macmillan, 1972.

Emmons, William H. *Gold Deposits of the World: With a Section on Prospecting.* Arno, 1974. (Reprint of McGraw-Hill edition, 1937.)

Fells, Peter D. *Gold.* (1969-1978). Report published annually by Consolidated Gold Fields, London.

Gold and World Monetary Problems. Proceedings of the National Industrial Conference Board convocation, Tarrytown, N.Y. New York: Macmillan, 1966.

Green, Timothy S. *The World of Gold Today.* New York: Walker, 1973.

Harrod, Sir Roy F. *Reforming the World's Money.* London: Macmillan, 1965.

Hayek, Friedrich A. *Choice in Currency: A Way to Stop Inflation.* Levittown, N.Y.: Transatlantic, 1977.

Hayek, Friedrich A. *Denationalization of Money.* London: Institute of Economic Affairs, 1976.

Hayek, Friedrich A. *Individualism and the Economic Order.* London: Routledge & Kegan Paul, 1976. (Reprint of 1958 ed.)

Hayek, Friedrich A. *Monetary Nationalism and International Stability.* Clifton, N.J.: Augustus M. Kelley, 1964. (Reprint of 1937 ed.)

Hayek, Friedrich A. *The Pure Theory of Capital.* Chicago: University of Chicago Press, 1975. (Reprint of Routledge ed., 1941.)

Hazlitt, Henry, ed. *The Critics of Keynesian Economics.* New Rochelle, N.Y.: Arlington House, 1977. (Reprint of Van Nostrand ed., 1960.)

Hazlitt, Henry. *What You Should Know About Inflation,* 2nd ed. New York: Van Nostrand Reinhold, 1965.

Jastram, Roy W. *The Golden Constant: The English and American Experience, 1560–1976.* New York: Wiley, 1977.

Meiselman, David I. and Arthur B. Laffer, eds. *The Phenomenon of Worldwide Inflation.* Washington: American Enterprise Institute, 1975.

Myers, C.V. *The Coming Deflation—Its Dangers and Opportunities.* New Rochelle, N.Y.: Arlington House, 1976.

Rees-Mogg, William. *The Reigning Error: the Crisis of World Inflation.* London: Hamilton, 1974.

Rothbard, Murray. *America's Great Depression,* rev. ed. Mission, Kansas: Sheed Andrews & McMeel, 1975.

Sutherland, Carol Humphrey Vivian. *Gold: Its Beauty, Power, and Allure.* 2nd rev. ed. New York: McGraw-Hill, 1969.

Triffin, Robert. *Gold and the Dollar Crisis: The Future of Convertibility,* rev. ed. New Haven: Yale University Press, 1961.

Von Mises, Ludwig. *Bureaucracy.* New Rochelle, N.Y.: Arlington House, 1969. (Reprint of 1944 ed.)

Von Mises, Ludwig. *Socialism.* Translated by J. Kahane. London: Jonathan Cape, 1951.

Von Mises, Ludwig. *The Theory of Money and Credit.* New York: Foundation for Economic Education, 1971.

Wilson, Francis. *Labour in the South African Gold Mines, 1936–1969.* London: Cambridge University Press, 1972.

Wise, Edmund M. *Gold: Recovery, Properties, and Applications.* Princeton, N.J.: Van Nostrand, 1964.

Gold Newsletters

The Bank Credit Analyst
Butterfield Building, Front St., Hamilton, Bermuda.
$275 per year/12 issues (A)

Barron's
22 Courtland St., New York, N.Y. U.S.A. 10007.
$42 per year/weekly (A) (B)

Harry Brown's Special Reports
P.O. Box 5586, Austin, Texas, U.S.A. 78763.
$175 per year. (A)

Deliberations
The Ian McAvity Market Letter
Box 182, Adelaide Street Station, Toronto, Ont. M5C 2J1.
$150 per year. (B)

Dow Theory Letter
P.O. Box 1759, La Jolla, California, U.S.A. 92037.
$125 per year. (B)

(A) Contains regular in-depth gold information, along with foreign exchange forecasts and general comments on the international monetary scene.

(B) Contains regular comments on gold and currency opportunities, along with stock-market analysis.

(C) Contains strictly gold information.

The Dyne's Letter
18E 41st St., New York, N.Y. U.S.A. 10017
$115 per year. (B)

International Reports
200 Park Avenue South, New York, N.Y. U.S.A. 10003.
$600 per year. (A)

Kiplinger Washington Newsletter, 1729 8th St. N.W., Washington,
   D.C. U.S.A. 20006.
$36 per year. (A)

Gold Newsletter
8422 Oak St., New Orleans, La. U.S.A. 70118.
$20 per year/monthly. (C)

Market Report*
87 Yonge Street, Toronto, Ontario M5C 1S8.
$25 per year/24 issues. (A)

Myer's Finance & Energy
Gottfried-Kellerstrasse 7, 8001 Zurich, Switzerland.
$162 per year. (A)

James Sinclair & Co.
90 Broad Street, New York, N.Y. U.S.A. 10004
$150 per year. (A)

World Money Analyst
1129 National Press Building, Washington, D.C. U.S.A. 20045.
$75 per year. (A)

*Market Report is published by Peter C. Cavelti

Complete Listing of Gold Coins

On the following pages, you will find a complete listing of gold coins minted since the year A.D. 1000. The study features the country and striking year for each coin. It also gives the gold content in ounces and the net value of the gold contained in each coin at different bullion prices. If the bullion price is at a level not described in our comparison, you can easily calculate the value yourself by multiplying the content by the current gold price.

Our comparison will greatly facilitate the calculation of coin premiums which, as we have seen in previous chapters, are the most vital factor in coin investment. When you have determined the gold value of a coin and compared it to its selling price, you have arrived at the premium. In order to work out the premium in percentage terms, divide the dealer's price by the gold value.

Let us use an example taken from the following page. You will notice that the 1 Habibi coin of Afghanistan is worth $36 at a bullion price of $300. If, at the time you make the comparison, the gold price is quoted at $315, this would bring the gold value of the piece to $38 ($315 x 0.122 ounces = $38.43). Now you find that your local coin dealer is charging $62 for the same piece. You are therefore paying a premium of $24 or 61.3% ($62–$38 = $24; $62 divided by $38.43 = 161.3 = premium of 61.3%).

All gold contents quoted on the following pages are rounded up or down to three decimals. All gold values are adjusted to the nearest U.S. dollar.

Country or Coin Area		Gold Content in oz.	Years Produced	Gold Value at: $ 200	$ 300	$ 400
Afghanistan	1 Tilla	0.133	1896-1919	26	39	53
	5 Amani	0.638	1921	127	191	255
	2 Amani	0.263	1921-1924	53	78	105
	1 Amani	0.132	1919-1932	26	39	53
	1/2 Amani	0.066	1921-1928	13	20	26
	21/2 Amani	0.434	1925-1928	86	130	173
	1 Amani	0.173	1925-1928	34	51	69
	1/2 Amani	0.087	1925-1928	17	25	34
	1 Habibi	0.122	1929	24	36	48
	20 Afghani	0.173	1929-1930	34	51	69
Africa	3 Dinars	0.395	660-1902	79	118	158
	2 Dinars	0.263	660-1902	52	78	105
	1 Dinar	0.132	660-1902	26	39	52
	1/2 Dinar	0.066	660-1902	13	20	26
	1/4 Dinar	0.033	660-1902	6	10	13
Ajman	100 Riyals	0.627	1970	125	188	251
	75 Riyals	0.449	1970	89	134	179
	50 Riyals	0.299	1970	62	94	125
	25 Riyals	0.149	1970	31	47	62
Albania	100 Francs	0.933	1926-1938	186	279	373
	50 Francs	0.467	1938	93	139	186
	20 Francs	0.187	1926-1938	37	56	74
	10 Francs	0.093	1927	18	28	37
	500 Leks	2.857	1968-1970	571	857	1142
	200 Leks	1.142	1968-1970	228	342	456
	100 Leks	0.571	1968-1970	114	171	228
	50 Leks	0.285	1968-1970	57	85	114
	20 Leks	0.114	1968-1970	22	34	45
Anguilla	100 Dollars	1.428	1967	285	428	571
	20 Dollars	0.285	1967	57	85	114
	10 Dollars	0.142	1967	28	42	57
	5 Dollars	0.071	1967	14	21	28
Argentina	5 Pesos	0.233	1881-1896	46	69	93
	21/2 Pesos	0.117	1881-1884	23	34	46
Asia	5 Mohurs	1.718	1200-1947	343	515	687
	2 Mohurs	0.687	1200-1947	137	206	274
	1 Mohur	0.344	1200-1947	68	103	137
	1/2 Mohur	0.172	1200-1947	34	51	68

Country or Coin Area		Gold Content in oz.	Years Produced	Gold Value at:		
				$ 200	$ 300	$ 400
Asia (cont.)	1/4 Mohur	0.086	1200-1947	17	25	34
	1/8 Mohur	0.043	1200-1947	8	12	17
	1/16 Mohur	0.021	1200-1947	4	6	8
	1/32 Mohur	0.011	1200-1947	2	3	4
	3 Dinars	0.395	660-1902	79	118	158
	2 Dinars	0.263	660-1902	52	78	105
	1 Dinar	0.132	660-1902	26	39	52
	1/2 Dinar	0.066	660-1902	13	20	26
	1/4 Dinar	0.033	660-1902	6	10	13
Austria	4 Ducats	0.443	1793-1915	88	132	177
	2 Ducats	0.221	1799-1804	44	66	88
	1 Ducat	0.111	1792-1915	22	33	44
	1 Soverain	0.327	1781-1800	65	98	130
	1/2 Soverain	0.163	1781-1800	32	49	65
	1 Sovrano	0.328	1820-1856	65	98	130
	1/2 Sovrano	0.164	1820-1856	32	49	65
	1 Krone	0.321	1858-1866	64	96	128
	1/2 Krone	0.161	1858-1866	32	48	64
	8 Florins	0.187	1870-1892	37	56	74
	4 Florins	0.093	1870-1892	18	28	37
	100 Corona	0.980	1908-1915	196	294	392
	20 Corona	0.196	1892-1912	39	58	78
	10 Corona	0.098	1892-1912	19	29	39
	100 Kronen	0.980	1923-1924	196	294	392
	20 Kronen	0.196	1923-1924	39	58	78
	100 Schilling	0.681	1926-1938	136	204	272
	25 Schilling	0.170	1926-1938	34	51	68
Bahamas	100 Dollars	1.177	1967-1971	235	353	471
	50 Dollars	0.588	1967-1971	117	176	235
	20 Dollars	0.235	1967-1971	47	70	94
	10 Dollars	0.116	1967-1971	23	35	47
	100 Dollars	0.941	1972	188	282	376
	50 Dollars	0.470	1972	94	141	188
	20 Dollars	0.188	1972	37	56	75
	10 Dollars	0.094	1972	18	28	37
	100 Dollars	0.273	1973	54	81	109
	50 Dollars (Crawfish)	0.136	1973	27	40	54
	50 Dollars (Flamingo)	0.294	1973	58	88	117
	20 Dollars	0.054	1973	10	16	21
	10 Dollars	0.027	1973	5	8	10

Country or Coin Area		Gold Content in oz.	Years Produced	Gold Value at:		
				$ 200	$ 300	$ 400
Bahamas (cont.)	200 Dollars	0.321	1974-1975	64	96	128
	150 Dollars	0.241	1974-1975	48	71	96
	100 Dollars (Independence)	0.289	1974-1975	58	86	115
	100 Dollars (4 Flamingoes)	0.160	1974-1975	32	49	64
	50 Dollars	0.080	1974-1975	16	24	32
Bahrain	10 Dinars	0.471	1968	94	141	188
Barbados	100 Dollars	0.099	1975	19	29	39
Belgium	100 Francs	0.933	1853-1912	186	279	373
	40 Francs	0.373	1834-1841	74	111	149
	25 Francs	0.233	1847-1850	46	69	93
	20 Francs	0.187	1835-1914	37	56	74
	10 Francs	0.093	1849-1912	18	28	37
Bermuda	20 Dollars	0.235	1970	47	70	94
	100 Dollars	0.226	1975	45	67	90
Bhutan	5 Sertums	1.178	1966	235	353	471
	2 Sertums	0.471	1966	94	141	188
	1 Sertum	0.235	1966-1970	47	70	94
Biafra	25 Pounds	2.354	1969	470	706	941
	10 Pounds	1.177	1969	235	353	471
	5 Pounds	0.470	1969	95	143	191
	2 Pounds	0.235	1969	47	70	94
	1 Pound	0.117	1969	23	35	47
Bolivia	1 Onza	1.041	1868	208	313	416
	35 Grams	1.125	1952	225	337	450
	14 Grams	0.450	1952	90	135	180
	7 Grams	0.225	1952	45	67	90
	3 1/2 Grams	0.113	1952	22	33	45
Botswana	10 Thebe	0.327	1966	65	98	130
	150 Pulce	0.471	1976	94	141	188
Brazil	4000 Reis	0.241	1695-1833	48	72	96
	2000 Reis	0.120	1695-1793	24	36	48
	1000 Reis	0.060	1695-1787	12	18	24
	20000 Reis	1.579	1724-1727	315	473	631

Country or Coin Area		Gold Content in oz.	Years Produced	Gold Value at:		
				$ 200	$ 300	$ 400
Brazil (cont.)	10000 Reis	0.789	1724-1727	157	236	315
	4000 Reis	0.315	1703-1727	63	94	126
	2000 Reis	0.158	1703-1727	31	47	63
	1000 Reis	0.079	1708-1727	15	23	31
	400 Reis	0.031	1725-1730	6	9	12
	12800 Reis	0.842	1727-1733	168	252	336
	6400 Reis	0.421	1727-1833	84	126	168
	3200 Reis	0.210	1727-1786	42	63	84
	1600 Reis	0.105	1727-1784	21	31	42
	800 Reis	0.052	1727-1786	10	15	21
	400 Reis	0.026	1730-1734	5	7	10
	20000 Reis	0.528	1849-1922	105	158	211
	10000 Reis	0.264	1849-1922	52	77	105
	5000 Reis	0.132	1854-1859	26	38	52
	300 Cruzeiros	0.492	1972	98	147	196
British Empire	5 Pounds	1.177	1817-1964	235	353	471
	2 Pounds	0.471	1817-1964	95	143	191
	1 Pound	0.235	1817-1964	47	70	94
	1/2 Pound	0.118	1817-1964	23	35	47
British Virgin Islands	100 Dollars	0.205	1975	41	61	82
Brunei	$1,000	1.472	1978	294	442	589
Bulgaria	100 Leva	0.933	1894-1912	186	279	373
	20 Leva	0.186	1894-1912	37	56	74
	10 Leva	0.093	1894	18	28	37
	20 Leva	0.488	1963-1964	97	146	195
	10 Leva	0.244	1963-1964	48	73	97
Burma	5 Rupees	0.101	1880	20	30	40
	4 Rupees	0.081	1852-1878	16	24	32
	2 Rupees	0.040	1852-1880	8	12	16
	1 Rupee	0.020	1852-1880	4	6	8
Burundi	100 Francs	0.925	1962	185	277	370
	50 Francs	0.463	1962	92	138	185
	25 Francs	0.2315	1962	46	67	92
	10 Francs	0.092	1962	18	27	37
	100 Francs	0.868	1965	173	260	347
	50 Francs	0.434	1965	86	130	173
	25 Francs	0.217	1965	43	65	86
	10 Francs	0.086	1965	17	26	34

Country or Coin Area		Gold Content in oz.	Years Produced	Gold Value at:		
				$ 200	$ 300	$ 400
Cameroun	20000 Francs	2.025	1970	405	607	810
	10000 Francs	1.013	1970	202	303	405
	5000 Francs	0.506	1970	101	151	202
	3000 Francs	0.303	1970	60	90	121
	1000 Francs	0.101	1970	20	30	40
Canada	5 Dollars	0.241	1912-1914	48	72	96
	10 Dollars	0.483	1912-1914	96	144	192
	20 Dollars	0.538	1967	105	158	211
	100 Dollars Olympic	0.241	1976	48	72	96
	100 Dollars Olympic	0.483	1976	96	144	192
	100 Dollars Jubilee	0.500	1977	100	150	200
	100 Dollars Unity	0.500	1978	100	150	200
	100 Dollars Year of Child	0.500	1979	100	150	200
	50 Dollars Maple Leaf	1.000	1979-	200	300	400
Cayman Islands	25 Dollars	0.253	1972	50	75	101
	100 Dollars	0.364	1974-1975	72	109	145
Central Africa	20000 Francs	2.025	1970	405	607	810
	10000 Francs	1.013	1970	202	303	405
	5000 Francs	0.506	1970	101	151	202
	3000 Francs	0.303	1970	60	90	121
	1000 Francs	0.101	1970	20	30	40
Central America	50 Pesos	0.578	1970	115	173	231
Chad	20000 Francs	2.025	1970	405	607	810
	10000 Francs	1.013	1970	202	303	405
	5000 Francs	0.506	1970	101	151	202
	3000 Francs	0.303	1970	60	90	121
	1000 Francs	0.101	1970	20	30	40
Chile	10 Pesos	0.439	1853-1890	87	131	175
	5 Pesos	0.219	1858-1873	43	65	87
	2 Pesos	0.088	1857-1875	17	26	35
	1 Peso	0.044	1860-1873	8	13	17

Country or Coin Area		Gold Content in oz.	Years Produced	Gold Value at:		
				$ 200	$ 300	$ 400
Chile (cont.)	20 Pesos	0.352	1896-1917	70	106	141
	10 Pesos	0.176	1895-1901	35	53	70
	5 Pesos	0.088	1895-1900	17	26	35
	100 Pesos	0.588	1926-1963	117	176	235
	50 Pesos	0.294	1926-1962	58	88	117
	20 Pesos	0.117	1926-1961	23	35	46
	500 Pesos	2.941	1967	588	882	1176
	200 Pesos	1.176	1967	234	352	470
	100 Pesos	0.588	1967	117	176	235
	50 Pesos	0.294	1967	58	88	117
China, Republic	20 Dollars	0.428	1919	86	128	172
	10 Dollars	0.214	1916-1919	43	64	86
China, Yunnan	10 Dollars	0.260	1919	52	78	104
	5 Dollars	0.130	1919	26	39	52
China, Nationalist	2000 Yuan	0.868	1965	174	261	348
	1000 Yuan	0.434	1965	87	130	174
	2000 Yuan	0.949	1966	190	285	380
Colombia	20 Pesos	0.933	1859-1877	187	280	373
	10 Pesos	0.467	1856-1877	93	140	186
	5 Pesos	0.233	1856-1885	46	70	93
	2 Pesos	0.098	1856-1876	19	28	37
	1 Peso	0.047	1856-1878	9	14	18
	1 Peso	0.471	1919-1924	94	35	47
	5 Pesos	0.235	1913-1930	47	71	94
	2 1/2 Pesos	0.118	1913-1928	23	35	47
	1500 Pesos	1.867	1968-1971	373	560	747
	500 Pesos	0.622	1968-1971	124	186	249
	300 Pesos	0.373	1968-1971	75	112	149
	200 Pesos	0.249	1968-1971	50	74	100
	100 Pesos	0.124	1968-1971	25	37	50
	1500 Pesos (Bank)	0.553	1973	111	166	221
	1500 Pesos (Valencia)	0.249	1973	50	74	100
	2000 Pesos	0.373	1973	75	112	149
	1000 Pesos	0.124	1973-1975	25	37	50
	1000 Pesos	0.249	1975	50	74	100
Costa Rica	10 Pesos	0.402	1870-1876	80	121	161
	5 Pesos	0.201	1867-1875	40	60	80

Country or Coin Area		Gold Content in oz.	Years Produced	Gold Value at:		
				$ 200	$ 300	$ 400
Costa Rica (cont.)	2 Pesos	0.081	1866-1876	16	24	32
	1 Peso	0.040	1864-1872	8	12	16
	20 Colones	0.450	1897-1900	90	135	180
	10 Colones	0.225	1897-1900	45	67	90
	5 Colones	0.113	1899-1900	23	33	45
	2 Colones	0.045	1897-1928	9	13	18
	1000 Colones	5.615	1970	1123	1685	2246
	500 Colones	2.156	1970	562	843	1123
	200 Colones	0.862	1970	224	336	448
	100 Colones	0.431	1970	112	168	224
	50 Colones	0.216	1970	56	84	112
	1500 Colones	0.968	1974	194	290	387
Croatia	500 Kuna	0.282	1941	56	85	113
Cuba	20 Pesos	0.967	1915-1916	193	290	387
	10 Pesos	0.484	1915-1916	96	145	193
	5 Pesos	0.242	1915-1916	48	72	96
	4 Pesos	0.193	1915-1916	39	58	77
	2 Pesos	0.097	1915-1916	21	29	37
	1 Peso	0.048	1915-1916	10	14	18
Czechoslovakia	10 Ducats	1.106	1929-1951	221	332	442
	5 Ducats	0.553	1929-1951	110	166	221
	5 Ducats (Commemorative)	0.634	1929	127	190	254
	4 Ducats	0.443	1928	89	133	177
	3 Ducats	0.380	1929	76	114	152
	2 Ducats	0.221	1923-1951	44	66	88
	1 Ducat	0.111	1923-1951	22	33	44
	1 Ducat (Commemorative)	0.127	1929	25	38	51
Dahomey	25000 Francs	2.572	1970	514	772	1029
	10000 Francs	1.029	1970	206	309	412
	4000 Francs	0.514	1970	103	154	206
	2500 Francs	0.257	1970	51	77	103
Danish West Indies	10 Daler	0.467	1904	93	140	187
	4 Daler	0.187	1904-1905	37	56	75
Danzig	25 Gulden	0.235	1923-1930	47	70	94
Denmark	2 Christian d'or	0.383	1826-1870	77	115	153

Country or Coin Area		Gold Content in oz.	Years Produced	Gold Value at:		
				$ 200	$ 300	$ 400
Denmark (cont.)	1 Christian d'or	0.191	1775-1869	38	57	76
	1 Courant Ducat	0.088	1771-1785	19	28	38
	1 Ducat	0.111	1771-1802	22	33	44
	10 Daler	0.467	1904	93	140	187
	4 Daler	0.187	1904-1905	37	56	75
	20 Kroner	0.259	1873-1931	52	78	104
	10 Kroner	0.130	1873-1917	25	39	52
Dominican Republic	30 Pesos	0.857	1955	171	257	343
	20 Pesos	0.338	1974	68	101	135
Ecuador	10 Sucres	0.235	1899-1900	47	71	94
	1 Condor	0.242	1926	48	73	97
Egypt	500 Piastres	1.196	1861-1960	239	359	478
	100 Piastres	0.239	1839-1960	48	72	96
	50 Piastres	0.120	1839-1958	24	35	48
	20 Piastres	0.048	1923-1938	10	14	20
	10 Piastres	0.024	1839-1909	2	3	5
	5 Piastres	0.012	1839-1909	2	3	5
	10 pounds	1.463	1964	293	439	585
	5 Pounds	0.731	1964	146	219	293
	1 Pound	0.239	1955-1960	48	72	96
	1 Pound	0.225	1970-1973	45	68	90
	1/2 Pound	0.120	1958	24	36	48
Ethiopia	2 Wark (± 14 grams)	0.405	1889-1917	81	122	162
	1 Wark (± 7 grams)	0.203	1889-1931	40	61	81
	1/2 Wark (± 3.5 grams)	0.101	1889-1931	20	30	40
	1/4 Wark (± 1.75 grams)	0.051	1889	10	15	20
	1/8 Wark (± 0.875 grams)	0.025	1889	5	7	10
	200 Dollars	2.315	1966	463	694	926
	100 Dollars	1.157	1966-1972	231	347	463
	50 Dollars	0.579	1966-1972	116	174	232
	20 Dollars	0.232	1966	46	70	93
	10 Dollars	0.116	1966	23	35	46
Europe	100 Ducats	11.063	1280-1960	2213	3319	4425
	50 Ducats	5.532	1280-1960	1106	1660	2213

Country or Coin Area		Gold Content in oz.	Years Produced	Gold Value at:		
				$ 200	$ 300	$ 400
Europe (cont.)	20 Ducats	2.213	1280-1960	443	664	885
	10 Ducats	1.106	1280-1960	221	332	442
	5 Ducats	0.553	1280-1960	111	166	221
	4 Ducats	0.443	1280-1960	89	133	177
	3 Ducats	0.332	1280-1960	66	100	133
	2 Ducats	0.221	1280-1960	44	66	88
	1 Ducat	0.111	1280-1960	22	33	44
	1/2 Ducat	0.055	1280-1960	11	17	22
	1/4 Ducat	0.028	1280-1960	6	8	11
	1/8 Ducat	0.014	1280-1960	3	4	6
	1/16 Ducat	0.007	1280-1960	1	2	3
	1/32 Ducat	0.003	1280-1960	.60	.90	1.2
Falkland Islands	5 Pounds	1.176	1974	235	353	470
	2 Pounds	0.471	1974	94	141	188
	Sovereign	0.0235	1974	47	71	94
	1/2 Sovereign	0.118	1974	24	35	47
Fiji	100 Dollars	0.504	1974	101	151	202
Finland	20 Markka	0.187	1878-1913	37	56	75
	10 Markka	0.093	1878-1913	19	28	37
	200 Markka	0.244	1926	49	73	98
	100 Markka	0.122	1926	24	37	49

France

The weight of French coins prior to 1803 fluctuated greatly. The gold contents and values quoted reflect averages.

		Gold Content in oz.	Years Produced	$ 200	$ 300	$ 400
	1 Ecu d'or	0.105	1266-1641	21	32	42
	1 Chaise d'or	0.151	1285-1422	30	45	60
	1 Royal d'or	0.135	1285-1461	27	41	54
	1 Lion d'or	0.158	1328-1350	32	47	63
	1 Pavillion d'or	0.164	1328-1350	33	49	66
	1 Ange d'or	0.233	1328-1350	47	70	93
	1 Mouton d'or	0.151	1350-1422	30	45	60
	1 Franc à cheval	0.125	1350-1461	25	38	50
	1 Franc à pied	0.123	1350-1380	25	37	50
	1 Salut d'or	0.125	1380-1461	25	38	50
	1 Heaume d'or	0.150	1380-1422	30	45	60
	1 Henry d'or	0.111	1550-1559	23	34	45
	2 Louis d'or	0.450	1640-1792	90	135	180
	1 Louis d'or	0.222	1640-1793	46	68	90
	1/2 Louis d'or	0.111	1640-1784	23	34	45
	100 francs	0.933	1855-1913	187	280	374

Country or Coin Area		Gold Content in oz.	Years Produced	Gold Value at:		
				$ 200	$ 300	$ 400
France (cont.)	50 francs	0.467	1855-1904	94	141	187
	40 francs	0.373	1803-1839	75	112	150
	20 francs	0.187	1803-1914	38	57	75
	10 francs	0.093	1854-1914	19	28	38
	5 francs	0.047	1854-1889	10	15	19
	100 francs	0.190	1929-1936	38	57	76
Fujairah	200 Ryials	1.200	1969	240	360	480
	100 Ryials	0.600	1969-1971	120	180	240
	50 Ryials	0.300	1970	60	90	120
	25 Ryials	0.150	1970	30	45	60
Gabon	100 Francs	0.926	1960	186	278	371
	50 Francs	0.463	1960	93	139	185
	25 Francs	0.232	1960	46	69	92
	10 Francs	0.093	1960	23	34	46
	20,000 Francs	2.025	1969	405	608	810
	10,000 Francs	1.013	1969	202	304	405
	5,000 Francs	0.506	1969	101	152	202
	3,000 Francs	0.304	1969	60	90	120
	1,000 Francs	0.101	1969	20	30	40
German East Africa	15 Rupees	0.217	1916	43	65	87
German New Guinea	20 Marks	0.231	1895	46	69	92
	10 Marks	0.115	1895	23	34	46
Germany	10 Taler	0.385	1742-1857	77	116	154
	5 Taler	0.192	1699-1856	38	58	77
	2¹/₂ Taler	0.096	1699-1855	19	29	38
	1 Pistole	0.192	1699-1856	38	58	77
	1 Frederick d'or	0.192	1699-1856	38	58	77
	1 Carolin	0.240	1726-1782	48	72	96
	¹/₂ Carolin	0.120	1726-1737	24	36	48
	¹/₄ Carolin	0.060	1726-1736	12	18	24
	4 Ducats	0.443	1797-1844	89	133	177
	2 Ducats	0.221	1768-1811	44	66	88
	1 Ducat	0.111	1764-1872	22	33	44
	2 Taler	0.077	1792-1830	15	33	31
	40 Francs	0.373	1813	75	112	149
	20 Francs	0.187	1808-1811	37	56	74
	10 Francs	0.093	1813	18	28	37
	5 Francs	0.047	1813	9	14	18

Country or Coin Area		Gold Content in oz.	Years Produced	Gold Value at:		
				$ 200	$ 300	$ 400
Germany (cont.)	10 Gulden	0.199	1819-1842	40	60	80
	5 Gulden	0.100	1819-1835	20	30	40
	1 Krone	0.321	1857-1871	64	96	128
	1/2 Krone	0.161	1857-1870	32	48	64
	15 Rupees	0.174	1916	35	52	70
	20 Marks	0.230	1871-1915	46	69	92
	10 Marks	0.115	1872-1914	23	34	46
	5 Marks	0.058	1877-1878	11	17	23
Ghana	5 Pounds	0.471	1960	94	141	188
Great Britain	*The weight of British coins prior to 1663 fluctuated greatly. The gold contents and values quoted reflect averages.*					
	1 Noble	0.251	1327-1483	50	75	100
	1 Angel	0.154	1422-1625	25	37	50
	1 Ryal	0.400	1485-1625	80	120	160
	1 Sovereign	0.384	1485-1525	77	115	154
	1 Sovereign	0.354	1526-1547	71	106	142
	1 Sovereign	0.384	1551-1625	77	115	154
	1 George Noble	0.133	1509-1547	23	35	46
	3 Pounds (Triple Unite)	0.796	1642-1644	159	239	318
	20 Shillings (One Unite)	0.265	1603-1663	53	80	106
	2 Crowns or 10 shillings	0.133	1603-1663	26	40	53
	1 Crown or 5 shillings	0.066	1509-1666	13	20	26
	1/2 Crown or 2 1/2 shillings	0.033	1509-1625	6	10	13
	5 Guineas	1.230	1668-1777	246	369	492
	2 Guineas	0.492	1664-1777	98	148	197
	1 Guinea	0.246	1663-1813	49	74	99
	1/2 Guinea	0.123	1669-1813	24	37	49
	1/3 Guinea	0.082	1797-1813	16	24	33
	1/4 Guinea	0.062	1718-1762	12	18	24
	5 Pounds	1.177	1820-1965	235	353	471
	2 Pounds	0.471	1820-1953	94	141	188
	1 Pound	0.235	1817-1966	47	70	94
	1/2 Pound	0.118	1817-1965	23	35	47
Greece	100 Drachmae	0.933	1876-1935	187	280	373
	50 Drachmae	0.467	1876	93	140	186

Country or Coin Area		Gold Content in oz.	Years Produced	Gold Value at:		
				$ 200	$ 300	$ 400
Greece	40 Drachmae	0.373	1852	46	70	93
(cont.)	20 Drachmae	0.187	1833-1935	23	35	46
	10 Drachmae	0.093	1876	11	17	23
	5 Drachmae	0.047	1876	5	8	11
Guatemala	20 Pesos	0.933	1869-1878	187	280	373
	16 Pesos	0.747	1863-1869	149	224	299
	10 Pesos	0.467	1869	93	140	186
	8 Pesos	0.373	1864	74	112	149
	5 Pesos	0.233	1869-1878	46	70	93
	4 Pesos	0.187	1861-1869	37	56	74
	2 Pesos	0.093	1859	18	28	37
	1 Peso	0.047	1859-1860	9	14	18
	4 Reales ($1/2$ Peso)	0.023	1859-1864	4	7	9
	20 Quetzales	0.967	1926	193	290	387
	10 Quetzales	0.484	1926	96	145	193
	5 Quetzales	0.242	1926	48	72	96
Guinea, Equ.	5000 Pesetas	2.041	1970	408	612	816
	1000 Pesetas	.408	1970	82	122	163
	750 Pesetas	0.306	1970	61	92	122
	500 Pesetas	0.204	1970	41	61	81
	200 Pesetas	0.102	1970	20	31	41
Guinea	10000 Francs	1.157	1969	231	347	463
	5000 Francs	0.579	1969-1970	115	173	231
	2000 Francs	0.232	1969-1970	46	70	92
	1000 Francs	0.116	1969	23	35	46
Haiti	1000 Gourdes	5.715	1967-1969	1142	1714	2286
	500 Gourdes	2.857	1968	571	857	1143
	250 Gourdes	1.429	1968	285	427	571
	200 Gourdes	1.143	1967-1971	228	343	457
	100 Gourdes	0.572	1967-1971	114	171	229
	60 Gourdes	0.371	1968	74	111	148
	50 Gourdes	0.286	1967-1971	57	85	114
	40 Gourdes	0.248	1968	46	68	92
	30 Gourdes	0.186	1968	37	55	74
	20 Gourdes	0.114	1967-1969	23	34	46
	1000 Gourdes	0.421	1973	84	125	168
	500 Gourdes	0.211	1973	42	64	84
	200 Gourdes	0.084	1973	16	26	34
	100 Gourdes	0.042	1973	8	13	17
	1000 Gourdes	0.379	1974	76	114	152

Country or Coin Area		Gold Content in oz.	Years Produced	Gold Value at:		
				$ 200	$ 300	$ 400
Haiti (cont.)	500 Gourdes	0.188	1974	38	57	76
	200 (Pope)	0.076	1975	15	23	30
	200 (Women)	0.085	1975	27	26	34
Hejaz	1 Dinar	0.213	1923	43	64	85
Honduras	20 Pesos	0.933	1888-1908	187	280	373
	10 Pesos	0.467	1871-1889	93	140	186
	5 Pesos	0.233	1871-1913	46	70	93
	1 Peso	0.047	1871-1922	9	14	19
	100 Lempiras	0.933	1971	187	280	373
	50 Lempiras	0.467	1971	93	140	186
	20 Lempiras	0.233	1971	46	70	93
	10 Lempiras	0.093	1971	19	28	37
Hong Kong	1000 Dollars					
	(Royal Visit)	0.471	1975	94	141	188
	(Dragon)	0.471	1976	94	141	188
	(Snake)	0.471	1977	94	141	188
	(Horse)	0.471	1978	94	141	188
	(Goat)	0.471	1979	94	141	188
	1 Ducat	0.111	1792-1831	22	33	44
	8 Forint	0.187	1870-1892	37	56	74
	4 Forint	0.093	1870-1892	18	28	37
Hungary	8 Florins	0.187	1870-1892	37	56	74
	4 Florins	0.093	1870-1892	18	28	37
	100 Korona	0.980	1907-1908	196	294	392
	20 Korona	0.196	1892-1918	39	59	78
	10 Korona	0.098	1892-1915	196	294	392
	100 Pengo	1.259	1938	252	378	504
	100 Pengo	0.839	1929-1938	168	252	336
	40 Pengo	0.336	1935	68	100	136
	20 Pengo	0.169	1928-1929	34	50	68
	10 Pengo	0.085	1928	17	25	34
	1000 Forint	2.433	1966	487	730	973
	500 Forint	1.111	1961	222	333	444
	500 Forint	1.217	1966	243	365	486
	200 Forint	0.487	1968	97	146	195
	100 Forint	0.222	1961	44	66	88
	100 Forint	0.243	1966	49	73	97
	50 Forint	0.111	1961	22	33	44
Iceland	10000 Kroner	0.449	1974	90	135	180

Country or Coin Area		Gold Content in oz.	Years Produced	Gold Value at:		
				$ 200	$ 300	$ 400
Iceland (cont.)	5000 Kroner	0.259	1961	52	78	104
India	200 Mohurs	68.73	1628-1658	13746	20619	27492
	100 Mohurs	34.365	1556-1707	6873	10130	13746
	5 Mohurs	1.718	1556-1627	344	515	687
	2 Mohurs	0.687	1556-1835	138	206	274
	1 Mohur	0.344	1200-1947	69	103	137
	1/2 Mohur	0.172	1200-1947	34	51	68
	1/3 Mohur	0.115	1200-1947	23	35	46
	1/4 Mohur	0.086	1200-1947	17	25	34
	1/6 Mohur	0.057	1500-1820	11	17	23
	1/8 Mohur	0.043	1500-1820			
	1/16 Mohur	0.022	1500-1820	5	8	11
	1/32 Mohur	0.011	1500-1820	2	4	5
	5 Rupees (1/3 Mohur)	0.115	1820-1879	23	35	46
	10 Rupees (2/3 Mohur)	0.230	1862-1879	46	70	92
	15 Rupees	0.235	1918	47	71	93
	1 Pagoda (primitive)	0.077	1200-1868	15	23	31
	2 Pagoda (modern) Madras	0.172	1810	34	52	69
	1 Pagoda (modern) Madras	0.086	1810	17	26	34
	2 Pagoda (modern) Travancore	0.150	1877-1924	30	45	60
	1 Pagoda (modern) Travancore	0.075	1877-1924	15	23	30
	1/2 Pagoda (modern) Travancore	0.038	1877-1924	7	11	15
	1/4 Pagoda (modern) Travancore	0.019	1877-1924	3	5	7
	100 Kori (Cuch Bhuj)	0.551	1866	110	165	220
	50 Kori (Cuch Bhuj)	0.276	1873-1874	55	82	110
	25 Kori (Cuch Bhuj)	0.138	1862-1870	28	41	55
Indonesia	25000 Rupiah	1.786	1970	357	536	714
	20000 Rupiah	1.429	1970	286	429	572

Country or Coin Area		Gold Content in oz.	Years Produced	Gold Value at:		
				$ 200	$ 300	$ 400
Indonesia	10000 Rupiah	0.714	1970	143	214	286
(cont.)	5000 Rupiah	0.357	1970	71	107	143
	2000 Rupiah	0.143	1970	29	43	57
	100000 Rupiah	0.967	1974	193	290	387
Iraq	5 Dinars	0.400	1971	80	120	160
Isle of Man	5 Pounds	1.177	1965	235	353	471
	1 Sovereign	0.235	1965	47	71	94
	1/2 Sovereign	0.118	1965	23	35	47
	5 Pounds	1.173	1973-1974	235	353	471
	2 Pounds	0.469	1973-1974	94	142	188
	1 Sovereign	0.235	1973-1974	47	71	94
	1/2 Sovereign	0.117	1973-1974	23	35	49
Israel	20 Pounds	0.235	1960	47	71	94
	100 Pounds	0.736	1962-1967	147	221	294
	50 Pounds	0.393	1962-1964	79	118	157
	100 Pounds	0.643	1968-1969	129	193	257
	100 Pounds	0.637	1971	127	191	255
	200 Pounds	0.781	1973	156	234	312
	100 Pounds	0.391	1973	78	117	156
	50 Pounds	0.203	1973	41	61	81
	500 Pounds	0.810	1974	162	243	324
	500 Pounds	0.579	1975	116	174	232
Italy	1 Doppia (2 Ducats)	0.222	1200-1815	44	67	89
	1 Genovino (1 Ducat)	0.111	1200-1415	22	33	44
	1 Florin (1 Ducat)	0.111	1250-1500	22	33	44
	1 Scudo d'oro (1 Ducat)	0.111	1300-1750	22	33	44
	1 Zecchino (1 Ducat)	0.111	1500-1800	22	33	44
	1 Zecchino, Florence (= 1 Ducat)	0.112	1712-1853	22	34	45
	1 Ruspone, Florence (= 3 Zecchini)	0.336	1719-1859	67	101	134
	80 Florins, Florence	1.049	1827-1828	210	315	420

Country or Coin Area		Gold Content in oz.	Years Produced	Gold Value at:		
				$ 200	$ 300	$ 400
Italy (cont.)	6 Ducats, Naples	0.248	1749-1785	50	74	99
	4 Ducats, Naples	0.165	1749-1782	33	50	66
	2 Ducats, Naples	0.827	1749-1772	165	248	331
	30 Ducats, Naples	1.213	1818-1856	243	364	485
	15 Ducats, Naples	0.606	1818-1856	121	182	242
	6 Ducats, Naples	0.243	1818-1856	49	73	97
	3 Ducats, Naples	0.121	1818-1856	24	36	48
Ivory Coast	100 Francs	0.926	1966	185	278	370
	50 Francs	0.463	1966	92	139	185
	25 Francs	0.232	1966	46	69	92
	10 Francs	0.926	1966	83	278	370
Jamaica	20 Dollars	0.253	1972	51	76	101
	100 Dollars	0.227	1975	45	68	91
Japan	20 Yen	0.965	1870-1880	193	289	386
	10 Yen	0.482	1871-1880	96	144	193
	5 Yen	0.241	1870-1897	48	72	96
	2 Yen	0.097	1870-1880	20	28	38
	1 Yen	0.048	1871-1880	10	14	19
	20 Yen	0.482	1897-1932	96	144	193
	10 Yen	0.241	1897-1910	48	72	96
	5 Yen	0.121	1897-1930	24	36	48
Jersey	50 Pounds	0.667	1972	133	200	267
	25 Pounds	0.351	1972	70	105	140
	20 Pounds	0.273	1972	55	82	109
	10 Pounds	0.137	1972	27	41	54
	5 Pounds	0.077	1972	13	20	27
Jordan	25 Dinars	2.000	1969	400	600	800
	10 Dinars	0.800	1969	160	240	320
	5 Dinars	0.400	1969	80	120	160
	2 Dinars	0.160	1969	32	48	64
Katanga	5 Francs	0.386	1961	77	116	154

Country or Coin Area		Gold Content in oz.	Years Produced	Gold Value at:		
				$ 200	$ 300	$ 400
Kenya	500 Shillings	1.120	1966	224	336	448
	250 Shillings	0.560	1966	112	168	224
	100 Shillings	0.224	1966	45	67	90
Korea	20 Won	0.482	1906-1910	96	145	193
	10 Won	0.241	1906-1910	48	72	96
	5 Won	0.121	1908-1909	24	36	48
Kuwait	5 Dinars	0.400	1961	80	120	160
Laos	80000 Kips	2.315	1971	463	695	926
	40000 Kips	1.157	1971	231	347	463
	20000 Kips	0.579	1971	115	173	231
	8000 Kips	0.232	1971	46	70	93
	4000 Kips	0.116	1971	23	35	46
	100000 Kips	0.219	1975	44	66	88
	50000 Kips	0.106	1975	21	32	42
Lesotho	20 Maloti	2.352	1966-1969	470	706	941
	10 Maloti	1.177	1966-1969	235	353	470
	4 Maloti	0.471	1966-1969	94	142	188
	2 Maloti	0.235	1966-1969	47	71	94
	1 Maloti	0.118	1966-1969	24	35	47
Liberia	20 Dollars (Red)	0.540	1964	108	162	216
	20 Dollars (Yellow)	0.599	1964	120	180	240
	30 Dollars	0.434	1965	87	130	174
	25 Dollars	0.675	1965	135	203	270
	12 Dollars	0.174	1965	35	52	70
	20 Dollars	0.968	1972	194	290	387
	10 Dollars	0.484	1972	97	145	198
	5 Dollars	0.242	1972	48	72	99
	2^{1}/2 Dollars	0.121	1972	24	36	49
Liechtenstein	20 Kronen	0.196	1898-1900	39	59	78
	10 Kronen	0.097	1898-1900	19	29	39
	20 Franken	0.187	1930-1946	37	56	75
	10 Franken	0.093	1930-1946	18	28	75
	100 Franken	0.933	1952	187	280	373
	50 Franken	0.327	1956-1961	65	98	131
	25 Franken	0.163	1956-1961	32	49	65

Country or Coin Area		Gold Content in oz.	Years Produced	Gold Value at:		
				$ 200	$ 300	$ 400
Luxembourg	20 Francs	0.187	1953	37	56	75
Malaysia	100 Ringgit	0.549	1971	110	165	220
Mali	100 Francs	0.926	1967	185	278	370
	50 Francs	0.463	1967	92	139	185
	25 Francs	0.232	1967	46	69	92
	10 Francs	0.093	1967	19	28	37
Malta	20 Scudi	0.432	1764-1778	86	130	173
	10 Scudi	0.216	1756-1782	43	65	86
	5 Scudi	0.108	1756-1779	21	32	43
	50 Pounds	0.965	1972	173	290	386
	20 Pounds	0.358	1972	72	107	143
	10 Pounds	0.177	1972	36	53	71
	5 Pounds	0.088	1972	18	26	35
	50 Pounds	0.442	1973-1975	88	133	177
	20 Pounds	0.177	1973-1975	36	53	71
	10 Pounds	0.088	1973-1975	18	26	35
Mauritius	200 Rupees	0.459	1971	92	138	184
	1000 Rupees	0.471	1978	94	141	188
Mexico	8 Escudos	0.762	1822	152	229	305
	8 Escudos	0.762	1823	152	229	305
	8 Escudos (Eagle)	0.762	1823	152	229	305
	8 Escudos (facing Eagle)	0.762	1824-1873	152	229	305
	4 Escudos	0.381	1823	76	114	152
	4 Escudos	0.381	1825-1869	76	114	152
	2 Escudos	0.190	1825-1870	38	57	76
	1 Escudo	0.095	1825-1870	19	29	38
	1/2 Escudo	0.048	1825-1869	9	14	19
	20 Pesos	0.952	1870-1905	190	286	381
	10 Pesos	0.476	1870-1905	95	143	190
	5 Pesos	0.238	1870-1905	47	71	95
	21/2 Pesos	0.119	1870-1893	23	35	47
	1 Peso	0.048	1870-1905	10	14	19
	50 Pesos	1.206	1921-1947	241	362	482
	20 Pesos	0.482	1917-1959	96	145	193
	10 Pesos	0.241	1905-1959	48	72	96
	5 Pesos	0.121	1905-1955	24	36	48

Country or Coin Area		Gold Content in oz.	Years Produced	Gold Value at:		
				$ 200	$ 300	$ 400
Mexico	2¹/₂ Pesos	0.060	1918-1948	12	18	24
(cont.)	2 Pesos	0.048	1919-1948	10	14	19
Monaco	40 Francs	0.373	1838	75	120	149
	100 Francs	0.933	1882-1904	187	280	373
	20 Francs	0.187	1838-1892	37	56	75
	2 Francs	0.463	1943	93	139	185
	1 Franc	0.231	1943	46	69	92
	100 Francs	0.738	1950	148	221	295
	100 Francs (Double)	1.476	1950	295	442	590
	50 Francs	0.593	1950	119	178	237
	50 Francs (Double)	1.186	1950	237	356	474
	20 Francs (Double)	0.420	1950	84	126	168
	20 Francs (Double)	0.839	1950	168	252	336
	10 Francs	0.304	1950	61	91	122
	10 Francs (Double)	0.608	1950	122	182	244
	100 Francs	0.347	1956	69	104	139
	200 Francs	0.947	1966	189	284	380
Montenegro	100 Perpera	0.980	1910	196	294	392
	20 Perpera	0.196	1910	39	59	78
	10 Perpera	0.098	1910	19	29	39
Morocco	4 Ryals	0.187	1879	37	56	75
	250 Dirham	0.187	1977	37	56	75
Muscat and Oman	15 Ryals	0.235	1962	47	70	94
Nepal	4 Mohars	0.679	1750-1938	136	204	272
	2 Mohars	0.340	1750-1938	68	102	136
	1 Mohar	0.170	1750-1938	34	51	68
	¹/₂ Mohar	0.085	1750-1938	17	25	34
	¹/₄ Mohar	0.042	1750-1911	8	13	17
	¹/₈ Mohar	0.021	1750-1911	4	6	8
	¹/₁₆ Mohar	0.011	1750-1911	2	3	4
	¹/₃₂ Mohar	0.005	1750-1911	1	1	2
	¹/₆₄ Mohar	0.003	1750-1911	1	1	2
	¹/₁₂₈ Mohar	0.001	1881-1911	0	0	0

Country or Coin Area		Gold Content in oz.	Years Produced	Gold Value at:		
				$ 200	$ 300	$ 400
Nepal (cont.)	2 Rupees	0.340	1948-1955	68	102	136
	1 Rupee	0.170	1938-1962	34	51	68
	1/2 Rupee	0.085	1938-1962	17	25	34
	1/4 Rupee	0.086	1955	17	25	34
	1/5 Rupee	0.069	1955	14	21	28
	1/6 Rupee	0.062	1956	12	19	25
Netherlands	14 Guilders	0.293	1749-1764	59	88	117
	7 Guilders	0.146	1749-1764	29	44	58
	20 Guilders	0.402	1808-1810	80	121	161
	10 Guilders	0.201	1808-1810	40	60	80
	20 Guilders	0.397	1848-1853	79	119	159
	10 Guilders	0.195	1818-1933	39	59	79
	5 Guilders	0.097	1826-1912	19	29	39
	1 Ducat	0.110	1960-1972	22	33	44
Netherlands East Indies	1 Ducat	0.110	1814-1937	22	33	44
Newfoundland	2 Dollars	0.098	1865-1888	19	29	39
Nicaragua	2000 Cordobas	0.500	1975	100	150	200
	1000 Cordobas	0.278	1975	56	83	111
	500 Cordobas	0.156	1975	31	47	62
	200 Cordobas	0.061	1975	12	18	24
Niger	100 Francs	0.926	1960-1968	185	278	370
	50 Francs	0.463	1960-1968	92	139	185
	25 Francs	0.232	1960-1968	46	70	92
	10 Francs	0.093	1960-1968	19	28	37
Norway	20 Kronor	0.259	1874-1910	52	78	104
	10 Kronor	0.130	1874-1910	26	39	52
Oman	500 Ryals	1.179	1971	236	354	476
	200 Ryals	0.472	1971	94	142	189
	100 Ryals	0.236	1971	47	71	94
	50 Ryals	0.118	1971	23	35	47
Ottoman Empire	5 Sequins	0.386	1451-1839	77	116	154
	4 Sequins	0.389	1451-1839	78	117	156
	3 Sequins	0.231	1451-1839	46	69	92
	2 Sequins	0.154	1451-1839	31	46	62
	1 Sequin	0.077	1451-1839	15	23	31
	1/2 Sequin	0.039	1451-1839	7	11	15

Country or Coin Area		Gold Content in oz.	Years Produced	Gold Value at:		
				$ 200	$ 300	$ 400
Panama	100 Balboas	0.236	1974	47	71	94
	500 Balboas	1.207	1975	241	361	483
Paraguay	10000 Guaranies	1.331	1968	266	399	532
	4500 Guaranies	0.923	1972-1974	185	277	369
	3000 Guaranies	0.616	1972-1974	123	185	246
	1500 Guaranies	0.310	1972-1974	61	82	123
Persia	1 Ashrafi	0.110	1500-1750	22	33	44
	25 Tomans	2.081	1848-1896	416	624	832
	20 Tomans	1.664	1848-1986	333	499	666
	20 Tomans	0.832	1848-1925	167	249	333
	5 Tomans	0.418	1848-1925	83	124	166
	2 Tomans	0.166	1848-1925	33	50	67
	1 Toman	0.083	1848-1927	16	25	33
	1/2 Toman	0.042	1848-1925	8	12	16
	1/5 Toman	0.017	1848-1925	3	5	7
	5 Pahlevi	0.278	1927-1930	56	83	111
	2 Pahlevi	0.111	1927-1930	22	33	44
	1 Pahlevi	0.056	1927-1930	11	16	22
	5 Pahlevi	1.177	1961-1975	235	353	471
	21/2 Pahlevi	0.589	1961-1975	118	177	236
	1 Pahlevi	0.235	1932-1975	47	71	94
	1/2 Pahlevi	0.118	1932-1975	23	35	47
	1/4 Pahlevi	0.059	1950-1975	11	17	23
	2,000 Rials	0.754	1971	151	226	302
	1,000 Rials	0.377	1971	74	113	151
	750 Rials	0.283	1971	57	85	113
	500 Rials	0.188	1971	23	35	47
Peru	20 Soles	0.933	1863	187	280	373
	10 Soles	0.467	1863	93	140	186
	5 Soles	0.233	1863	46	70	93
	1 Libra	0.235	1898-1964	47	71	94
	1/2 Libra	0.118	1902-1964	24	35	47
	1/5 Libra	0.047	1906-1964	9	14	19
	50 Soles	0.968	1930-1931	194	290	388
	100 Soles	1.354	1950-1969	271	406	542
	50 Soles	0.677	1950-1969	135	203	271
	20 Soles	0.271	1950-1969	54	81	108
	10 Soles	0.135	1956-1969	27	40	54
	5 Soles	0.68	1956-1969	13	20	27
Philippines	4 Pesos	0.190	1861-1882	38	57	76

Country or Coin Area		Gold Content in oz.	Years Produced	Gold Value at:		
				$ 200	$ 300	$ 400
Philippines (cont.)	2 Pesos	0.095	1861-1868	19	28	38
	1 Peso	0.048	1861-1868	9	14	19
	1 Piso	0.570	1970	114	171	228
	1000 Pisos	0.288	1975	57	85	114
Poland	1 Ducat	0.111	1812-1831	22	33	44
	50 Zloty	0.289	1817-1829	58	87	116
	25 Zloty	0.144	1817-1833	29	43	58
	20 Zloty (3 Roubles)	0.109	1834-1840	22	33	44
	20 Zloty	0.187	1925	37	56	75
	10 Zloty	0.093	1925	18	28	37
Portugal	4 Cruzados	0.444	1580-1652	89	133	178
	2 Cruzados	0.222	1580-1647	44	66	89
	1 Cruzado	0.111	1438-1647	22	33	45
	4000 Reis	0.316	1663-1722	63	95	126
	2000 Reis	0.158	1663-1725	31	47	63
	1000 Reis	0.079	1663-1821	16	23	31
	400 Reis	0.032	1717-1821	6	9	13
	8 Escudos	0.843	1717-1732	16	253	337
	4 Escudos	0.422	1722-1835	84	126	169
	2 Escudos	0.211	1722-1831	42	63	84
	1 Escudo	0.105	1722-1821	21	31	42
	1/2 Escudo	0.053	1722-1821	10	15	21
	5000 Escudos	0.282	1836-1851	56	85	113
	2500 Escudos	0.141	1838-1853	28	42	56
	1000 Escudos	0.070	1851	14	21	28
	10000 Escudos	0.523	1878-1889	105	157	209
	5000 Escudos	0.261	1860-1889	52	78	104
	2000 Escudos	0.105	1856-1888	21	32	42
	1000 Escudos	0.052	1855-1879	10	16	21
Ras Al Khaima	200 Riyals	1.198	1970	240	359	479
	150 Riyals	0.899	1970	180	270	360
	100 Riyals	0.599	1970	120	179	239
	75 Riyals	0.449	1970	90	135	180
	50 Riyals	0.300	1970	60	89	119
Rhodesia	5 Pounds	1.177	1966	235	353	471
	1 Pound	0.235	1966	47	71	94
	10 Shillings	0.118	1966	23	35	47
Romania	100 Lei	0.933	1906-1940	187	280	373

Country or Coin Area		Gold Content in oz.	Years Produced	Gold Value at:		
				$ 200	$ 300	$ 400
Romania (cont.)	50 Lei	0.467	1906-1922	93	140	186
	25 Lei	0.233	1906-1922	46	70	93
	20 Lei	0.187	1867-1944	37	56	75
	12$^{1}/_{2}$ Lei	0117	1906	24	35	47
Russia	25 Roubles	0.964	1876	193	289	386
	10 Roubles	0.384	1836	77	115	154
	5 Roubles	0.193	1826-1885	38	57	77
	3 Roubles	0.115	1826-1885	23	35	46
	10 Roubles	0.373	1886-1894	75	111	149
	5 Roubles	0.187	1886-1894	37	56	75
	15 Roubles	0.373	1897	75	111	149
	7$^{1}/_{2}$ Roubles	0.187	1897	37	56	75
	37$^{1}/_{2}$ Roubles	0.933	1902	187	280	373
	25 Roubles	0.933	1896-1908	187	280	373
	10 Roubles	0.249	1898-1923	50	75	100
	5 Roubles	0.125	1897-1910	25	37	50
	100 Roubles (Olympic)	0.500	1979-1980	100	150	200
Rwanda	100 Francs	0.868	1965	174	260	347
	50 Francs	0.434	1965	87	130	173
	25 Francs	0.217	1965	43	65	86
	10 Francs	0.087	1965	17	26	35
Salvador	20 Pesos	0.933	1892	187	280	373
	10 Pesos	0.467	1892	93	140	187
	5 Pesos	0.233	1892	46	70	93
	2$^{1}/_{2}$ Pesos	0.117	1892	23	35	46
	20 Colones	0.450	1925	90	135	180
	200 Colones	0.683	1971	137	205	273
	100 Colones	0.341	1971	68	102	136
	50Colones	0.171	1971	4	51	68
	25 Colones	0.085	1971	17	25	34
San Marino	20 Lire	0.187	1925	37	56	75
	10 Lire	0.093	1925	18	28	37
	2 Scudi	0.177	1974	35	53	71
	1 Scudo	0.088	1974	17	26	35
Saudi Arabia	4 Saudi Pounds	0.942	1945-1946	188	283	377
	1 Saudi Pound	0.235	1951-1957	47	71	94
Senegal	100 Francs	0.926	1968	185	278	370

Country or Coin Area		Gold Content in oz.	Years Produced	Gold Value at:		
				$ 200	$ 300	$ 400
Senegal	50 Francs	0.463	1968	92	139	185
(cont.)	25 Francs	0.232	1968	46	69	92
	10 Francs	0.093	1968	19	28	37
Serbia	20 Dinars	0.187	1879-1882	38	56	75
	10 Dinars	0.093	1882	19	28	38
Sharjah	200 Riyals	1.200	1970	240	360	480
	100 Riyals	0.600	1970	120	180	240
	50 Riyals	0.300	1970	60	90	120
	25 Riyals	0.150	1970	30	45	60
Siam	8 Ticals	0.227	1851-1868	46	68	91
	4 Ticals	0.113	1851-1868	23	34	46
	2 Ticals	0.057	1851-1907	12	17	23
Sierra	1 Golde	1.578	1966	316	474	631
Leone	1/2 Golde	0.789	1966	158	237	316
	1/4 Golde	0.395	1966	79	119	158
Singapore	150 Dollars	0.736	1969	147	221	295
	500 Dollars	1.000	1975	200	300	400
	250 Dollars	0.500	1975	100	150	200
	100 Dollars	0.200	1975	40	60	80
Somalia	500 Shillings	2.026	1965-1970	405	608	811
	200 Shillings	1.013	1965-1970	203	304	406
	100 Shillings	0.506	1965-1970	102	152	203
	50 Shillings	0.253	1965-1970	51	76	102
	20 Shillings	0.127	1965-1970	26	38	51
South	1 Pound	0.235	1874-1902	47	71	94
Africa	1/2 Pound	0.118	1892-1897	24	36	48
	1 British Sovereign	0.235	1923-1960	47	71	94
	1/2 British Sovereign	0.118	1923-1960	24	36	47
	2 Rand	0.235	1961-1964	47	71	94
	1 Rand	0.118	1961-1964	24	36	48
	1 Krugerrand	1.000	SINCE 1967	200	300	400
South Korea	25000 Won	2.801	1970	560	840	1120
	20000 Won	2.240	1970	482	723	964
	10000 Won	1.120	1970	224	336	448
	5000 Won	0.560	1970	112	168	224

Country or Coin Area		Gold Content in oz.	Years Produced	Gold Value at:		
				$ 200	$ 300	$ 400
South Korea (cont.)	2000 Won	0.280	1970	56	84	112
	1000 Won	0.112	1970	23	34	45
Spain	10 Doblas	1.106	1350-1369	222	332	443
	5 Doblas	0.713	1454-1474	143	237	286
	1 Dobla	0.143	1252-1474	29	43	58
	1/2 Dobla	0.071	1454-1474	15	22	29
	1 Excélente	0.111	1476-1516	23	34	45
	8 Escudos	0.796	1516-1772	160	239	319
	4 Escudos	0.398	1516-1772	80	120	160
	2 Escudos	0.199	1516-1772	40	60	80
	1 Escudo	0.099	1516-1772	20	30	40
	8 Escudos	0.781	1773-1785	157	235	313
	4 Escudos	0.391	1773-1785	79	118	157
	2 Escudos	0.195	1773-1785	39	59	78
	1 Escudo	0.098	1773-1785	20	30	39
	8 Escudos	0.076	1786-1833	152	228	304
	4 Escudos	0.380	1786-1833	76	114	152
	2 Escudos	0.190	1786-1833	38	57	76
	1 Escudo	0.095	1786-1833	19	29	38
	320 Reales	0.760	1810-1823	152	228	304
	160 Reales	0.380	1822	76	114	152
	80 Reales	0.190	1809-1848	38	57	76
	100 Reales	0.242	1850-1868	49	73	97
	40 Reales	0.097	1861-1868	20	29	39
	20 Reales	0.048	1861-1865	10	15	20
	100 Pesetas	0.933	1870-1897	187	280	374
	25 Pesetas	0.233	1871-1885	47	70	94
	20 Pesetas	0.187	1889-1904	38	56	75
	10 Pesetas	0.093	1878	19	28	38
Spanish America	8 Escudos	0.760	1598-1873	152	228	304
	4 Escudos	0.380	1598-1873	76	114	152
	2 Escudos	0.190	1598-1873	38	57	76
	1 Escudo	0.095	1598-1873	19	29	38
	1/2 Escudo	0.066	1598-1873	13	20	27
Swaziland	1 Lilangeni	0.836	1968	167	251	334
	25 Emalangeni	0.804	1974	161	241	322
	20 Emalangeni	0.643	1974	129	193	257
	10 Emalangeni	0.322	1974	64	97	129
	5 Emalangeni	0.161	1974	32	48	64
Sweden	1 Ducat	0.111	1793-1868	22	33	44

Country or Coin Area		Gold Content in oz.	Years Produced	Gold Value at:		
				$ 200	$ 300	$ 400
Sweden (cont.)	2 Ducats	0.221	1836-1857	44	66	88
	1 Carolin (10 francs)	0.093	1868-1872	19	28	37
	20 Kronor	0.259	1873-1925	52	78	104
	10 Kronor	0.130	1873-1901	26	39	52
	5 Kronor	0.065	1881-1920	13	20	26
Switzerland	24 Münzgulden	0.442	1794-1796	88	133	177
	12 Münzgulden	0.221	1794-1796	44	66	88
	6 Duplonen	1.326	1794	265	398	530
	4 Duplonen	0.884	1797-1798	177	265	354
	2 Duplonen	0.442	1793-1798	88	133	177
	1 Duplonen	0.221	1787-1829	44	66	88
	1/2 Duplonen	0.111	1787-1796	22	33	44
	1/4 Duplonen	0.006	1789-1796	1	2	2
	32 Franken	0.442	1800	88	133	177
	16 Franken	0.221	1800-1813	44	66	88
	8 Franken	0.111	1813	22	33	44
	20 Francs (Geneva)	0.183	1848	37	55	73
	10 Francs (Geneva)	0.092	1848	18	28	37
	20 Francs	0.093	1871-1947	19	28	37
	10 Francs	0.187	1911-1922	37	56	75
	100 Francs	0.933	1925	187	280	373
	100 Francs	0.749	1934	150	225	300
	100 Francs	0.506	1939	101	152	202
Syria	1 Pound	0.195	1950	39	59	78
	1/2 Pound	0.098	1950	20	29	39
Tanzania	1500 Shillings	0.968	1974	19	29	39
Thailand	600 Baht	0.434	1968	87	130	174
	300 Baht	0.217	1968	43	65	87
	150 Baht	0.109	1968	22	33	44
	800 Baht	0.579	1971	116	174	232
	400 Baht	0.289	1971	58	88	116
Tonga	1 Koula	0.959	1962	192	288	384
	1/2 Koula	0.479	1962	96	144	192
	1/2 Koula	0.240	1961	48	72	96
Tunis	100 Piastres	0.564	1855-1864	113	169	226
	80 Piastres	0.451	1855	90	135	180
	50 Piastres	0.282	1855-1867	56	85	113

Country or Coin Area		Gold Content in oz.	Years Produced	Gold Value at:		
				$ 200	$ 300	$ 400
Tunis (cont.)	40 Piastres	0.226	1855	45	68	90
	20 Piastres	0.141	1857-1882	28	42	56
	10 Piastres	0.113	1855	23	34	45
	5 Piastres	0.056	1855-1871	11	17	22
	2¹/₂ Piastres	0.028	1864-1872	6	8	11
	20 Francs	0.187	1891-1928	37	56	75
	15 Francs	0.140	1886-1891	28	42	56
	10 Francs	0.093	1891-1928	19	28	37
	100 Francs	0.190	1930-1955	38	57	76
Tunisia	40 Dinars	2.200	1967	440	660	880
	20 Dinars	1.100	1967	220	330	440
	10 Dinars	0.550	1967	110	165	220
	5 Dinars	0.275	1967	55	83	110
	2 Dinars	0.110	1967	22	33	44
Turkey	5 Sequins	0.386	1703-1839	77	116	154
	4 Sequins	0.309	1703-1839	62	93	124
	3 Sequins	0.232	1703-1839	46	70	93
	2 Sequins	0.154	1703-1839	31	46	62
	1 Sequin	0.077	1451-1839	15	23	31
	¹/₂ Sequin	0.039	1451-1839	78	117	156
	¹/₄ Sequin	0.019	1451-1839	4	6	8
	500 Piastres	1.063	1839-1975	213	319	425
	250 Piastres	0.532	1839-1975	106	160	213
	100 Piastres	0.213	1839-1975	43	64	75
	50 Piastres	0.106	1839-1975	21	32	42
	25 Piastres	0.053	1839-1975	11	16	21
	12¹/₂ Piastres	0.027	1909-1918	5	8	11
	500 Piastres (deluxe)	1.034	SINCE 1926	207	310	414
	250 Piastres	0.517	SINCE 1926	103	155	207
	100 Piastres	0.207	SINCE 1926	41	62	83
	50 Piastres	0.103	SINCE 1926	21	31	41
	25 Piastres	0.052	SINCE 1926	10	16	21
	500 Lire	0.177	1973	35	53	71
Turks & Caicos Islands	100 Crowns	0.290	1974	58	87	116
	50 Crowns	0.145	1974	29	44	58
	100 Crowns	0.200	1975	40	60	80
	50 Crowns	0.100	1975	20	30	40
	25 Crowns	0.050	1975	10	15	20
Tuvala	50 Dollars	0.471	1976	94	141	188

Country or Coin Area		Gold Content in oz.	Years Produced	Gold Value at:		
				$ 200	$ 300	$ 400
Uganda	1000 Shillings	4.000	1969	800	1200	1600
	500 Shillings	2.000	1969	400	600	800
	100 Shillings	0.400	1969	80	120	160
	50 Shillings	0.200	1969	40	60	80
Um-Al-Qawain	200 Riyals	1.200	1970	240	360	480
	100 Riyals	0.600	1970	120	180	240
	50 Riyals	0.300	1970	60	90	120
	25 Riyals	0.150	1970	30	45	60
United States of America	10 Dollars	0.516	1795-1804	102	153	204
	5 Dollars	0.258	1795-1833	52	77	103
	2$1/2$ Dollars	0.129	1796-1833	26	39	52
	5 Dollars	0.242	1834-1836	48	73	97
	2$1/2$ Dollars	0.121	1834-1836	24	36	48
	10 Dollars	0.483	1838-1933	97	145	193
	5 Dollars	0.242	1837-1929	48	73	97
	2$1/2$ Dollars	0.121	1837-1929	24	36	48
	20 Dollars	0.968	1850-1933	194	290	387
	3 Dollars	0.145	1854-1889	29	44	58
	1 Dollar	0.048	1849-1889	10	14	19
	4 Dollars	0.194	1879-1880	39	58	78
	50 Dollars	2.419	1915	484	726	968
Uruguay	5 Pesos	0.250	1930	50	75	100
Vatican	4 Doppia	0.631	1786-1787	126	189	252
	2 Doppia	0.315	1776-1777	63	95	126
	1 Doppia	0.158	1776-1834	32	47	63
	$1/2$ Doppia	0.079	1776-1787	16	24	32
	10 Scudi	0.501	1835-1856	100	150	200
	5 Scudi	0.250	1835-1854	50	75	100
	2$1/2$ Scudi	0.125	1835-1863	25	38	50
	1 Scudo	0.050	1853-1865	10	15	20
	100 Lire	0.933	1866-1870	187	280	373
	50 Lire	0.467	1868-1870	93	140	187
	20 Lire	0.187	1866-1870	37	56	75
	10 Lire	0.093	1866-1869	19	28	37
	5 Lire	0.047	1866-1867	9	14	19
	100 Lire	0.255	1929-1935	51	77	102
	100 Lire	0.150	1936-1959	30	45	60
Venezuela	100 Bolivares	0.933	1875-1889	187	280	373
	50 Bolivares	0.467	1875-1888	93	140	187

Country or Coin Area		Gold Content in oz.	Years Produced	Gold Value at:		
				$ 200	$ 300	$ 400
Venezuela (cont.)	25 Bolivares	0.233	1875	47	70	93
	20 Bolivares	0.187	1879-1912	37	56	75
	10 Bolivares	0.093	1930	19	28	37
	5 Bolivares	0.047	1875	9	14	19
Yemen Arab Republic	50 Ryals	1.418	1969	284	425	567
	30 Ryals	0.851	1969	170	255	340
	20 Ryals	0.567	1969	113	170	227
	10 Ryals	0.284	1969	57	85	114
	5 Ryals	0.142	1969	28	43	57
Yugoslavia	20 Dinars	0.187	1925	37	56	75
	1000 Dinars	2.263	1968	453	679	905
	500 Dinars	1.131	1968	226	339	452
	200 Dinars	0.453	1968	91	136	181
	100 Dinars	0.226	1968	45	68	90
Zanzibar	5 Rials	0.242	1881	48	73	97
	2$1/2$ Rials	0.121	1881	24	36	48

Index